Contents

List of illustrations	7
Preface	9
1. Of shipwrecks and economies	13
2. Myths, misconceptions and maritime heritage	23
3. Site-formation analyses	34
4. The shipwrecks of Byzantine Palestine	45
5. Specialised production in the Holy Land	74
6. Exports, imports and the balance of trade	93
7. Shipwreck archaeology: an integrated future	125
Bibliography	133
Index	155

To Sally

I could be a rich merchant in a fine bazaar.
But I'd rather be happy staring at a star...

Illustrations

Fig. 1. The harbours and anchorages of Byzantine Palestine [p. 20]
Fig. 2. LR5 bag-shaped amphora necks from the late sixth-century AD Dor D wreck typify levels of cargo amphora preservation off Israel [p. 25]
Fig. 3. Byzantine ships wrecked between the offshore islets and shore in the southern anchorage at Dor [p. 37]
Fig. 4. Surface manifestations of the Dor D shipwreck with ballast overlying wooden planking [p. 38]
Fig. 5. Plan of scattered hull planking from the Dor D shipwreck [p. 40]
Fig. 6. Hull planking from the Dor D shipwreck [p. 41]
Fig. 7. Plan of the sixth-century Tantura A hull from Dor [p. 42]
Fig. 8. Decorative bronze synagogue plaque from a seventh-century AD cargo in Atlit bay [p. 49]
Fig. 9. A pickaxe and hammer head and from wrecks Dor D and F respectively [p. 53]
Fig. 10. Copper flask and cooking-pot from the wrecks Dor A and Dor G [p. 53]
Fig. 11. White marble mortar from wreck Dor A [p. 55]
Fig. 12. Arms and lower shanks of encrusted Byzantine iron anchors from wreck Dor J [p. 57]
Fig. 13. Greek inscriptions on the collars of two steelyards from wreck Dor G [p. 60]
Fig. 14. Schematic drawing of a side section of a second-century AD Roman hull [p. 63]

Illustrations

Fig. 15. Schematic drawing illustrating the general change in mortise-and-tenon ship joinery between the late fourth century BC, the fourth century AD, the seventh century AD and the ninth century AD [p. 64]

Fig. 16. Wooden hull planking amongst ballast stones from wreck Dor D, with an unpegged tenon protruding from its mortise [p. 66]

Fig. 17. Distribution map of Byzantine wine presses in Israel (excluding the Negev) [p. 87]

Fig. 18. A Byzantine wine press from Tel Qasile, with a reconstructed wooden screw apparatus in the treading-floor [p. 89]

Fig. 19. Plan of a fourth-century wine press with screw system from Jalame [p. 90]

Fig. 20. Fourth- or fifth-century wine press with screw system from the Jewish village of Sumaqa [p. 91]

Fig. 21. Palestinian LR4 and LR5 bag-shaped amphorae [p. 95]

Fig. 22. Distribution map of Palestinian amphorae exported from the Holy Land, fourth to seventh centuries AD [p. 97]

Fig. 23. Byzantine LR1 imported amphorae found in Israel: Caesarea, Scythopolis, Tel Masos, Jerusalem, Caesarea and Ashdod [p. 103]

Figs 24-28. Imported Byzantine amphorae found in Israel [pp. 104, 106, 107, 108 & 109]

Fig. 29. Distribution map of Phocaean Red Slip bowls imported into Byzantine Palestine from Asia Minor [p. 111]

Preface

Wherever there's hope of profit
Our merchant fleet will venture, will sail beyond Crete or
 Rhodes or
Past the Moroccan coastline, leaving Gibraltar behind them...
It's a fine return for such labours to sail back home in triumph,
Purse full, moneybags bursting, with tales to tell of the wonders
You encountered en route – not least those husky young mermen.
Delusions take various forms.
Juvenal, Satire 14

The threat of shipwreck and its implications have challenged Mediterranean societies for millennia. A guild of Roman *urinatores* (divers) based at the port of Ostia was trained to salvage cargoes lost in the Mediterranean, while satirists like Juvenal used the shipwreck genre as a source of immense tragi-comedy, considering the quest for profit at any cost and shipwrecked mariners begging on the streets of the Eternal City more entertaining than the theatre or religious festivals. Just how the subject vexed the minds of Byzantine legislators is evident from sections dealing with salvage in the seventh-century AD Rhodian Sea Law.

In eras when sea passage offered the only means of efficient communication, material and oral, the status of the ship was pre-eminent. Despite acute awareness of the moods of the Mediterranean, formalised in Antiquity in the writing of *periploi* (nautical handbooks), which charted offshore hazards,

Preface

winds, currents and reliable anchorages, ships always foundered in enormous quantities between Antiquity and the Early Modern era. In the first millennium BC Mediterranean and Black Seas alone, loss rates may well have exceeded 15,000 ships (Bascom 1987: 222-3).

By the early 1990s, 1,200 shipwrecks had been recorded in the Mediterranean and Roman provinces (Parker 1992a). There is no question that this is the tip of an immense iceberg. The waters of Greece, for example, hold an additional estimated 1,000 wrecks, almost none of which have been published. With 95% of the sea inaccessible by conventional diving using an aqualung, these figures will soar as the use of robotic Remotely Operated Vehicles, capable of plunging well beyond 1,000 m, increases.

Archaeology has always been a sampling exercise. Just as no sane archaeologist would attempt to excavate an entire ancient city (the toil of centuries), so scholars of the maritime realm must be selective in deciding which shipwrecks to excavate. Similarly, as coastal development continues to consume coastlines through the building of marinas and offshore pipelines, countries will need to tailor Cultural Resource Management to realistic and specific objectives. Not every ancient ship can be saved for mankind – the costs of preserving intact hulls and well-preserved cargoes are massive. Although an extreme case, the *Mary Rose* project cost £6.5 million between 1979 and 1985 (Harrison 2003: 66-7) and in 2002 received a further £4.2 million from the United Kingdom's Heritage Lottery Fund for the second phase of the ship's conservation. Meanwhile, £3.5 million has been earmarked to preserve the fifteenth-century Newport Ship abandoned on the banks of the River Usk, Wales, £1.5 million of which will be required to treat the timbers alone.

When confronted with these pressures of an ever-expanding world, deciding what precise form of information we require from our maritime heritage is of paramount importance and a

Preface

question of delicate balance. This is the philosophy that underlies this book: how to maximise our knowledge of Antiquity through the application of efficient methodologies. The debate is framed by examining a very high-profile province as a case study: the Byzantine Holy Land (fourth to seventh centuries AD), which became a 'flagship' of the Eastern Empire with the rise of Constantinople and adoption of Christianity as the official state religion. Throughout this process of exploration we analyse just what questions we should be demanding of the shipwreck heritage and the relevance of such enquiry.

In the writing of this book I am most grateful for the encouragement of Professor Richard Hodges, Deborah Blake and Duckworth. This book incorporates substantial unpublished data from my doctoral thesis at the University of Oxford (Kingsley 1999a) and I remain extremely appreciative of the wisdom, advice and humour offered by the late John Lloyd, Bryan Ward-Perkins, Claudine Dauphin and Martin Goodman, and of the support provided by Somerville College. Professor Dauphin has also very generously allowed the use of unpublished quantitative data in this book based on her excavations at Dor and Ohad in Israel. The comparative material incorporated was procured from eighteenth- to early twentieth-century travelogues in the Palestine Exploration Fund, where Rupert Chapman and Shimon Gibson kindly facilitated access. Sincere appreciation is also extended to Oxford's Byzantinists, who taught me the appropriateness of contextualising shipwrecks historically and of reaching out to embrace a variety of sources. This book was written under a Visiting Fellowship to the Research Centre for Late Antique and Byzantine Studies at the University of Reading, where I am grateful to Ken Dark. Peter Clayton kindly cast a knowledgeable eye over this text.

This book is dedicated to my sister Sally with love and respect for a brave woman who, unlike so many of us, has always lived very much in the present, not in the past or future.

1

Of shipwrecks and economies

Introduction

From the fantastic fiction of Jules Verne to eerie photographs of the *Titanic*, shipwrecks and the deep sea exert a potent influence over our imagination and historical consciousness. Within mainstream archaeology, however, shipwreck studies have long been an area of acute specialism. Until the 1980s the discipline's potential and objectives were marginalised by many classical archaeologists, some of whom patronised the subject as of dubious scientific importance. Meanwhile, many marine archaeologists did little to win round their colleagues, restricting their publications to obscure journals and failing to present and share their results in mainstream archaeology conferences.

Since the early 1980s, however, when George Bass wrote of his frustration at continuously having to defend shipwreck archaeology, a misunderstood science (Bass 1983), there has been a change in the academic climate. The split over the superior quality of respective sources that once divided archaeologists and classicists was an academic teething tantrum that has now largely been outgrown. Optimising our knowledge of a fragmentary antiquity, it is now accepted, demands that we weave together sources from all the disparate disciplines: archaeology, history, epigraphy, papyrology, even philosophy. Social archaeology's ongoing focus on everyday life in antiquity, reflected in the centrality of exchange and economics as key fields of Roman and Late Roman research (Storey 1999: 223-31), has been accompanied by increased interest in shipwrecks as tools for examining trade patterns.

Several high-profile shipwreck excavations have exerted an important influence over mainstream archaeology. With its cargo of copper and tin ingots, combined with a culturally diverse array of merchants' seals and other belongings, the late fourteenth-century BC Ulu Burun shipwreck off Turkey lies at the heart of contemporary studies of Late Bronze Age exchange dynamics and Canaanite society (Bass 1991). The cargo of 800 Etruscan commercial amphorae excavated off southern France on the Grand Ribaud A shipwreck of *c.* 600 BC (Long and Sourisseau 2002) has confounded scholars' former interpretation of the period's seaborne trade as dominated by elite exchange. Yassi Ada A, a ship wrecked in AD 625/6 off southern Turkey, remains crucial to contemporary debate about the extent to which state-dominated exchange or entrepreneurial commerce prevailed in Late Antiquity (van Alfen 1996). In the last 50 years shipwreck studies have challenged and changed our preconceptions about the character, organisation and scale of trade, and the extent to which ancient societies relied on non-local products. Nowhere is this clearer than in Parker's ground-breaking synthesis of 1,200 shipwrecks from the Mediterranean and Roman provinces (Parker 1992a), which provides invaluable quantitative data for holistic research into the ebb and flow of Roman and Byzantine inter-regional trade.

Shipwreck archaeology has also experienced a leap in potential during the last 15 years through the application of Remote Operated Vehicle (ROV) technology, which promises access to thousands of shipwrecks lying in the abyss at depths of over 1,000 m. Unpublished Punic wrecks have been plotted in the Straits of Gibraltar; a small Late Roman merchant vessel has been surveyed at Skerki Bank between Carthage and Sicily

1. Of shipwrecks and economies

(where it had ignored conventional wisdom by cutting a corner across the open sea; McCann and Freed 1994); and an intact vessel of c. AD 400, complete with rope still wound around an intact mast, has been recorded in the Black Sea (Ballard *et al.* 2001). The future of shipwreck archaeology has arrived.

Analytical versus intuitive approaches

Ancient shipwrecks are now attested as far afield as the Erythraean Sea (Pedersen 2000) and Dover. A diverse array of Greek, Roman and Byzantine produce has been identified, from cargoes of Hellenistic statues at Porticello to a pre-fabricated Late Roman church at Marzamemi, as well as fleets of wrecks containing thousands of amphorae. Archaeologists have compiled extensive data on ancient shipbuilding techniques and have related ship size and construction methods to the social hierarchies underlying trade management.

It is neither in regard to excavation and survey methodology, nor in relation to the quality of some outstanding fieldwork and publications that shipwreck archaeology is susceptible to criticism. My concerns lie in the conceptualisation and application of the theoretical frameworks underlying most research designs, which remain primarily site-specific rather than being devised to examine specific historical issues. Given the unbalanced chronological and typological spread of ships recorded in the Mediterranean, the school of 'historical particularism' (Bass 1983: 98, 103-4) has argued that in the current climate emphasis must be laid on the detailed excavation and research of individual sites to serve as missing links for specific periods. All true and wise. Yet for shipwreck archaeology to fulfil its potential and to become appropriately integrated within mainstream archaeology, it seems to me that the discipline needs to evolve significantly by shifting its research designs from being predominately intuitive to more analytical.

Shipwreck Archaeology

Much current fieldwork is initiated in order to record wrecks from under-represented or as yet unattested centuries, or is embedded within cultural resource management programmes (e.g. coastal development; combating treasure-hunting) that are chronologically pluralistic in application. Artefact recovery and site recording take precedence over wreck date or historical context. Such projects are obviously essential to safeguard national heritage and are entirely justified in their own right. However, alongside the successful planning of hulls and characterisation of cargoes, the majority of projects make no attempt to relate sites to regional forms of specialised agricultural and industrial production, to consumer nodes (geographic and social), or to the political economies that stimulated shipping in different periods. Instead, unbalanced emphasis is placed on the quest for well-preserved wrecks rather than on sites that hold the potential to unlock complex historical problems. This approach is as artificial as focusing solely on dominant archaeological sites in a landscape at the expense of rural infrastructure (farms, field irrigation systems, plough-zone sherd scatters as indications of changing agricultural intensity over time) as if 'cities' encapsulate all information required to interpret ancient settlement patterns.

The ships of Antiquity did not sail in a cultural vacuum. For shipwreck archaeology to become fully integrated into the writing of long-term history, it is essential to relate individual wrecks, and wreck clusters with repetitive cargo types, to regional provinces and localised production traditions. It is necessary to examine the contexts (urban, rural, elite, middle-class) in which shipped produce was consumed. Examining an ancient shipwreck in archaeological isolation is the equivalent of attempting to read poetry or appraise a painting in the absence of any bibliographic profile of the poet or artist. Of course, such literature and art will speak to us at one level, but without clarifying the context or the true meaning intended. If

1. Of shipwrecks and economies

archaeology is science, in the long term such an isolationist approach is unacceptable to shipwreck studies.

Integrated trade models: Spain, North Africa and Rome

Implementation of the holistic approach advocated above will succeed or fail on the basis of numerous inter-related factors, especially national attitudes to recording cultural heritage, excavation history, and accessibility of published reports. Primarily it relies on levels of archaeological knowledge concerning regional patterns of town and country relations, a comprehensive example of which is the trade in oil and grain exported from Spain and North Africa to Rome as *annona civica* (state-controlled dole derived from taxation in kind).

Historical sources suggest that about 200,000 citizens were eligible for free wheat and oil in Rome during the first century AD. Such demand resulted in an estimated 60 million *modii*, or 400,000 tons of wheat, being imported from Egypt and North Africa (Casson 1980: 21), an amount which would have required a minimum of 800 annual shipments in a vessel transporting 340 tons of cargo (Rickman 1980: 263). An equally important resource for the Eternal City was olive oil. Until the late second century AD, Baetica in southern Spain met most of its demands: Spanish Dressel 20 vessels comprise an estimated 80-85% of the amphorae from Monte Testaccio (some 3.7 tons of oil), that huge hill of discarded sherds in Rome (Mattingly 1988b: 54). This research can be tied to archaeological surveys conducted in the Guadalquivir Valley in Andalucia in southern Spain (Mattingly 1988b: 41-2), where a minimum of 150-200 mid-second-century kilns may have operated in a region where groves may have sustained an annual yield of between 20,000 and 100,000 tons of olives.

North Africa supplanted Baetica as the prime supplier of

Rome's olive oil during the third century AD, when an estimated 10 million olive trees were cultivated within the Sahel region of Tunisia (Mattingly 1988b: 44-5). The countryside around Lepcis Magna in modern Libya was a second epicentre of this agricultural activity and may have produced 20 million litres of exportable oil yearly, the equivalent of 350,000 full amphorae (Mattingly 1988a: 27).

The combined evidence of stamps placed on the necks of many Tunisian amphorae, which are abbreviated names of leading Lepcitanian families, and the capital investment required to finance large agricultural estates where olives were cultivated and oil processed, suggests that olive oil production for the *annona* may originally have been organised by the elite as a means of securing imperial patronage (Mattingly 1988a: 35). The structural change in amphora production identified in the Sahel region of Tunisia, where potteries relocated from coastal cities and towns to inland rural estates during the first half of the fifth century, may indicate that by this time rural produce was no longer packaged for the state in centralised, urban contexts (Peacock *et al.* 1989: 199-200). The argument for greater commercial penetration in North Africa's oil industry is implicit in the presence of batches of African Red Slip oil lamps and dishes excavated from various Late Roman shipwrecks off southern France and destined for the open market. The state even seems to have deliberately encouraged entrepreneurship by allowing the treasury to sell on surplus North African oil tax to Spain through commercial channels (Keay 1984: 417).

Integrated trade models: the Byzantine Holy Land

Serious methodological weaknesses exist in the data harnessed in the Rome/North Africa *annona* trade model: there is an over-dependence on statistics procured from historical sources, notoriously problematic and impossible to verify inde-

1. Of shipwrecks and economies

pendently; the North African oil production chronology is largely based on generalised dates for oil presses and olive groves; too few shipwrecks have been examined to contribute to the model, especially off North Africa; a far clearer profile is required of the penetration of African Red Slip fine-ware bowls and plates throughout the western Mediterranean in order to appraise the extent to which the *annona* sea-lanes were exploited for commercial gain.

As an alternative case study, therefore, one particular high-profile province in one historical period will be discussed to demonstrate the parameters of shipwreck archaeology: the Byzantine Holy Land (*c.* AD 320-640; Fig. 1). The reasons for this choice are manifold. Primarily, rescue excavations triggered by Israel's modern building boom have led to extensive archaeological data emerging for the Byzantine period. Although research conducted into the 1970s retained a strong religious orientation, concentrating on Jewish and Christian religious structures (synagogues, churches, monasteries, pilgrimage sites, hermits' cells), subsequent secular archaeology has recorded a remarkable diversity of Byzantine structures and landscapes in detail, unparalleled in any other East Mediterranean province.

Byzantine Palestine incorporates the territory of the three *Palaestinae* (*Prima, Secunda* and *Tertia*) of Byzantine civil, military and ecclesiastical administration. The borders of different countries are today imposed over these provinces, with the result that archaeological traditions and knowledge differs for the region. This study encompasses modern Israel from Mount Hermon in the north to the Sinai Desert in the south, the Mediterranean Sea to the west and River Jordan and Dead Sea to the east. The arid lands of South-West Jordan are excluded.

At least 2,930 Byzantine sites have been registered across Israel (Dauphin 1998: 51). Results from more than 22 regional

Shipwreck Archaeology

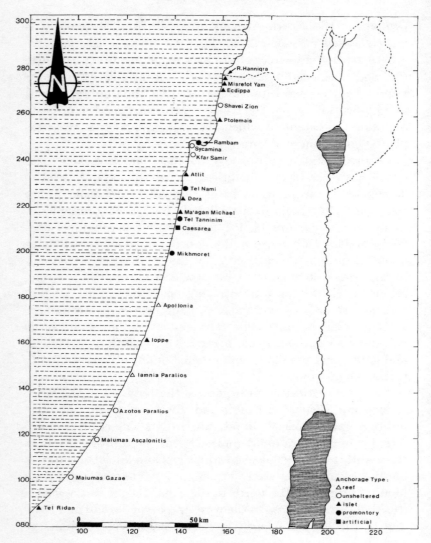

Fig. 1. The harbours and anchorages of Byzantine Palestine.

1. Of shipwrecks and economies

surveys are available from diverse zones ranging from the arid Negev Desert reliant on flash-flood farming for subsistence to the fertile Jezreel Valley and southern Shefarim foothills, which benefit from an average annual rainfall of 500-700 mm. Comparisons between quantities of Roman and Byzantine sites published in survey reports consistently indicate extreme growth in land exploitation in Late Antiquity. In northern Israel numbers of sites rise by between 30% and 105%. In the Gazit region of Galilee a 205% increase in settlement occurred, and in parts of the Negev site volumes increase from three to 95 sites. On average, sites present in Byzantine Palestine increased by 170% in relation to the preceding Roman period (Kingsley 1999a: 36-8).

The conundrum of the size of Byzantine Palestine's population remains hotly debated, with estimates varying from one million (Broshi 1979: 5) to 2.3 million (Felix, cited in Tsafrir 1996: 270); the former is generally accepted, but future research may well prove the figure to be on the low side. As with other parts of the Empire, society was largely rural, with between 17-20% of the population inhabiting Palestine's 25 cities (Hirschfeld 1997: 37; Safrai 1994: 103).

For purposes of trade studies, extensive excavations conducted at the coastal cities of Apollonia, Dor, Caesarea, Ashkelon and Gaza have provided key information about amphora dates, origins and scales of import. The character of rural production (in particular wine, oil and dye processing) is also well understood as a result of the publication of the nation-wide fieldwork of the Archaeological Survey of Israel, coupled with more intensive, independent landscape surveys. Numerous amphora kilns studied between the Galilee and Gaza regions enable specific local vessel variants to be dated and provenanced with precision. Finally, underwater surveys conducted off Israel since the 1960s have yielded extensive primary data. The city of Dor, in particular, is internationally renowned for the eight Byzantine shipwrecks within its southern harbour (Kingsley and Raveh 1996; Wachsmann and Kahanov 1997; Kingsley 2002; Mor 2002-3).

The objective of this book is to draw on largely unknown sources relating to Byzantine Palestine to freshly appraise the value of Mediterranean shipwrecks as primary sources for understanding ancient societies and their economies. Because so little has been published about the economy of the Holy Land and on evidence for maritime trade, substantial primary data is presented in order to frame agendas for debate. Chapters 2 and 3 investigate myths and misconceptions of ancient Palestinian shipping and argue that although the Holy Land's maritime history was rich and varied, appraisals of the reasons why vessels foundered and in what volume are sorely naïve; consequently, both cultural resource management and academia possess an inaccurate view of shipwreck archaeology. Chapter 4 contains core data about the shipwrecks of the Holy Land and discusses socio-economic patterns and qualitative problems that impede interpretation. Chapter 5 reverts to dry land to examine the regional forms of specialised production revealed through settlement archaeology (wine, cloth, dye and glass production) and examines how this data dovetails or differs from the shipwreck data. Finally, Chapter 6 focuses on the profiles that best explain the Holy Land's maritime trade. Local and imported amphorae and fine ware bowls prove the most superior sources available for formulating models. Throughout, it is argued vehemently that the study of shipwrecks as isolated sites is artificial and a detriment to the writing of long-term history.

2

Myths, misconceptions and maritime heritage

Holy Land, unholy sea?

Before aviation revolutionised travel to and from Israel in the twentieth century, seafaring was the only efficient means of inter-regional communication for more than 3,000 years. To modern society, with its easily satisfied wanderlust and bustling international airports, where quick-fix shops overflow with the fruits of globalisation, the enduring cultural vibrancy of a traditional maritime community is not easily imagined. Echoes of the jostling mercantile quarters that linked coastal Palestine with the wider world come to life today only in pockets of heritage zones, such as coastal Akko and Jaffa (ancient Ptolemais and Ioppe), preserved and revitalised for tourist appeal.

Appreciation of the scope of the Holy Land's maritime tradition has witnessed a slow and sceptical awakening. The roots of modern misconceptions date back to the first century AD, when Josephus Flavius described Palestine as 'not a maritime country, neither commerce nor the intercourse which it promotes with the outside world has any attraction for us ...' (*Against Apion* 1.60; St Thackeray 1966: 187). On the basis of this commentary Roman Palestine is often assumed to have comprised an economically introverted province reliant on subsistence farming and small-scale localised industry. This view was emphasised in the last decade of the nineteenth century when the pioneering historical geographer, George

Adam Smith, concluded that most of the linear, harbourless Holy Land (Fig. 1) was 'merely a shelf for the casting of wreckage and the roosting of sea-birds. ... It seemed as if the land were everywhere saying to the sea: I do not wish you, I do not need you. And this echoes through most of the Old Testament. Here the sea spreads before use for spectacle, for symbol, for music, for promise, but never for use ...' (Smith 1894: 128, 131-2). In the absence of river estuaries, sheltered coves, gulfs and major natural harbours, Smith assumed that geographical determinism conditioned economic reality.

Biased by perceptions of ritual purity underlying Jewish laws of food preparation and consumption (whereby orthodox Jews eat only from ceramic vessels whose purity can be guaranteed; cf. Magness 2002: 76-9), Israel's schools strongly promoted this non-maritime view of regional history well into the second half of the twentieth century. Such ideology almost certainly also underlined the argument that the predominant type of amphora in Roman and Byzantine Palestine, a short, bag-shaped vessel (see LR5 in Chapters 4-5; Figs 2, 21), was neither designed for, nor suited to sea-borne trade (Zevulin and Olenik 1979: 28). This was extended to apply to ancient Palestinian society in general, even to Late Antiquity when Christianity predominated.

The commercial marketing of scuba (self-contained underwater breathing apparatus) from 1948 onwards is widely credited with having breathed life into marine archaeology, laying to rest the myth of Palestine's lack of maritime history. Marine archaeology developed in Israel in the 1960s and 1970s, when research concentrated mainly on ancient harbours whose artificial structural remains were relatively easily identifiable along shorelines and in shallow waters: the breakwaters of Roman Caesarea were surveyed in 1960 by the Link Expedition (Fritsch and Ben-Dor 1961), the threat of a new fishing port under construction at Akko resulted in the Phoenician, Roman

2. Myths, misconceptions and maritime heritage

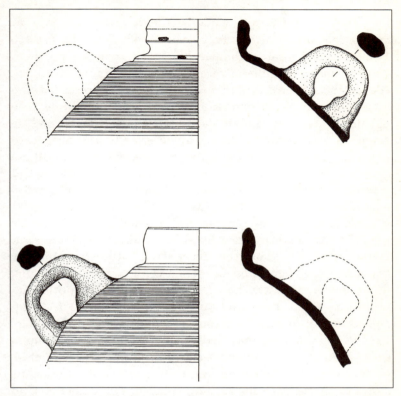

Fig. 2. LR5 bag-shaped amphora necks from the late sixth-century AD Dor D wreck typify levels of cargo amphora preservation off Israel.

and medieval breakwaters being recorded from 1964-6 (Flinder *et al.* 1993), and from 1965-6 the Undersea Exploration Society of Israel studied the Phoenician harbour of Atlit (Raban and Linder 1993: 117-20).

During this pioneering phase of exploration, shipwreck archaeology experienced a frustrating identity crisis. Well-preserved shipwrecks, typically characterised by a dense concentration of intact amphorae overlying a wooden hull, were turning up by the dozen in surveys off southern France, Italy and Turkey, and were considered the optimum site type for excavation and study. Surveys conducted along the coast of Israel failed to locate a comparable wreck, though large quantities of intact amphorae recovered in fishing trawlers' nets (Barag 1963) offered tantalising hints that well-preserved shipwrecks must await detection. However, these came from offshore waters up to 65 m deep (Zemer 1977: 1), beyond the range of contemporary diving apparatus. In the absence of accessible sites, it was, ironically, the well-preserved hull and cargo of an eighteenth-century merchant vessel located off Sharm el Sheikh in the Sinai that became the first wreck excavated by an Israeli team (Raban 1971).

Marine archaeology came of age in Israel during the 1970s. In 1972 the Institute for Maritime Studies was founded at Haifa University (now the Recanati Institute for Maritime Studies), establishing an academic context for the fledgling discipline. In 1976 the Israel Department of Antiquities and Museums (now the Israel Antiquities Authority: IAA) appointed a unit to record the country's underwater archaeology. In this decade of innocence, most fieldwork involved developing excavation and recording methods during the seasonal survey of new sites that had been naturally uncovered after winter storms from beneath the region's ephemeral blankets of sand. Particularly important shipwrecks excavated in subsequent decades include the 35-m-long Roman shipwreck at north Caesarea (Fitzgerald 1994), a Roman fishing boat on the shores of the Sea of Galilee (Wachsmann 1990), the Ma'agan Michael shipwreck of c. 400 BC (Linder 1993), and eight Byzantine and one Abassid shipwreck at Dor (Kingsley and Raveh 1996; Wachsmann et al. 1997; Kingsley 2002). Today, IAA records hold information on 200 shipwrecks and cargoes located mainly at depths of 1-6 m, 60-200 m offshore (Galili 1992: 23, 26). Estimates suggest that wrecks exist every 25-50 m along the country's 230 km-long coastline (Wachsmann 1984-5: 25; Galili 1992: 23).

2. Myths, misconceptions and maritime heritage

Maritime heritage and modern misconceptions

While the continuing study of Phoenician, Roman and Byzantine ports and shipwrecks has now enabled the scope of Palestine's maritime history to be reconceived, other misconceptions and problems have arisen instead. Developed, academically-driven shipwreck archaeology continues to make Israel one of the hot-spots for the discipline. However, the vast majority of sites among the body of 200 wrecks are not discovered and studied by university projects, but by the marine unit of the Israel Antiquities Authority (henceforth IAA), whose primary emphasis is cultural resource management.

A major dilemma conditioning IAA fieldwork is site looting, to the extent that combating this issue through rapid survey, recording and artefact recovery has been identified as the main priority of fieldwork strategies. According to official figures, 60% of all archaeological material existing on wreck sites off Israel has been looted (Galili and Sharvit 1992: 273). With one of the largest diving communities in the world (35,000 registered divers), the IAA's two full-time marine archaeologists simply do not have the resources to monitor winter wreck exposure and unlicensed intervention.

While the seriousness of this problem must not be undervalued, various inaccuracies currently characterise this rationalisation of IAA strategy. Three prevailing misconceptions and problems surround shipwreck archaeology in Israel:

(i) Scuba revolutionised shipwreck archaeology.
(ii) 60% of all existing wreck finds have been recovered illegally.
(iii) Within 10-20 years' time very little shipwreck heritage will survive underwater (Galili and Sharvit 1992: 273).

Debate concerning these issues is currently virtually non-existent, but without open discussion the character and scale of ancient shipwrecks as a national cultural resource, and matters of qualifying how to manage this resource, will remain undeveloped. Strong new evidence is introduced below to propose that the above points are misleading, resulting in skewed contemporary perception and thus inappropriate management.

Coastal development and wreck exposure

Technologically, the impact of the aqualung on the marine archaeology of the Holy Land cannot be exaggerated in terms of its success in facilitating unrestricted access to the seabed for extensive periods of time. But it was not the prime mover behind the inception of shipwreck archaeology. If scuba had been marketed in 1900, rather than 48 years later, divers would have observed little more than a startled array of marine wildlife. It is more accurate to say that shipwreck archaeology has emerged in Israel in the wake of extensive coastal development, which has triggered massive erosion of beaches and offshore sediments, and exposed countless wreck sites.

Until 1964 beach sand was quarried at an annual rate that is estimated to have exceeded by 10-20 times that naturally replenished by longshore sediment transport deposition. The result has been a huge sand deficit along Israel's central coastline, causing accelerated erosion of beaches and coastal cliffs. Such quarrying may have stripped Israel's beaches of one-third of its total sand reserves (Nir 1982a: 1839, 1846).

Since 1965 over 30 structures (detached breakwaters, groynes, sea-walls, marinas, small ports) have been built along the coastline mainly for recreational purposes (Nir 1990: 211). Regrettably, much of this construction irresponsibly neglected the consequent impact on the marine environment in the form of downshore erosion. Thus, the Carmel beaches almost completely disappeared following the construction of a detached breakwater at Haifa (Nir 1982a: 1846). Construction of the port

2. Myths, misconceptions and maritime heritage

of Ashdod interrupted 80-90% of the annual northward sand transport, estimated at 50,000-100,000 m^3 yearly (Nir 1982b: 91). To the north the sand-starved beaches of Yavne-Yam (Byzantine Iamnia Paralios) have withdrawn by about 50 m over the last 50 years (Nir 1982a: 1843).

The thinning of underwater sand blankets off Israel (Ashkelon to Haifa) is a recognised phenomenon. Consequent cases of extensive wreck exposure include Late Bronze Age, Late Roman and Byzantine cargo assemblages recorded off Sdot Yam (Galili *et al.* 1993) and the 19 shipwrecks dating between the twelfth century BC and the Ottoman period at Dor (Kingsley and Raveh 1996; Wachsmann and Davis 2002: 508-15; Kahanov 2002-3). The construction of the Hadera power plant (with offshore cooling pools) seems to have been more than a contributing trigger behind the exposure of maritime deposits at both sites. More astonishingly, for decades underwater surveys in the Roman and Byzantine port of Apollonia failed to reveal any significant maritime material culture. Only in 1991, following the ambitious construction of a large marina at Herzeliyah, did remains of submerged colonnaded storerooms with tessellated floors and Roman and post-medieval wreckage emerge (Grossmann 2001). Archaeological material recovered off Ashkelon has been exposed following the construction of the city's marina and expansion of the existing harbour (Galili *et al.* 2001). Coastal development, of course, is an essential industry for the social and economic vitality of a high-profile tourist Mediterranean destination like Israel, but for maritime heritage has proven a double-edged sword.

Quantifying shipwreck losses

The twin evils of random wreck exposure and apparent rampant looting are alleged to be so extreme that by about 2012 little of Israel's shipwreck heritage will remain preserved underwater. Although this comment is based on the extensive fieldwork and accumulated wisdom of IAA archaeologists, it remains nevertheless a highly contentious conclusion. Just how reliable is this worrying estimate? What means of objectively assessing the scale of shipwreck losses in antiquity are available?

Fortunately, nineteenth-century historical records offer detailed comparative insights into shipping conditions along a coastline whose geomorphology has remained largely unchanged since the limited riverine harbours silted up at the end of the Late Bronze Age (c. 1100 BC), leaving the coastal ports as the primary maritime gateways into Palestine (Raban 1985: 26). Irrespective of technological improvements – specifically, the use of sturdy steamers with anchor chains of iron rather than rope – relatively small wooden ships remained the dominant mode of transport for regional East Mediterranean trade until the early twentieth century. The wooden ship in which J.S. Buckingham sailed from Egypt to Syria in 1815 was typical of much maritime traffic of the period. With three masts and a crew of ten men and one captain, this *shuktoor* transporting corn and rice had a 40-ton capacity (Buckingham 1821: 3). Customs records verify that in 1894, 66 steamers and 991 sailing ships passed through Akko; 36 steamers and 691 sailing ships visited the same port in 1913 (Kark 1990: 81). Observations recorded at the port of Jaffa, where the beaches were 'thickly strewn with the wrecks of vessels of all nations and sizes, from the fine English barque of 400 hundred tons to the insignificant Arab felucca' (Neale 1852: 81), prove that a wide variety of craft were equally susceptible to regional storms.

During the nineteenth century shipwreck was considered one of the nightmares of the age, and an intense fascination with the subject has created a rich source of comparative data for reconstructing aspects of the precarious lifestyles of mercantile communities. The interest in wrecks between 1815 and 1840, in particular, was not merely an expression of Romantic

2. Myths, misconceptions and maritime heritage

sensitivity, although starry-eyed wonder at the antiquity of the Holy Land is patently perceptible in many travelogues. Repetition of maritime activities recorded in different media (by writers, artists and finally photographers) demonstrates the factual content at the heart of most of these nineteenth- and early twentieth-century records.

Wreck-spotting was particularly popular in the nineteenth century. Cunningham Geikie reported 'a galley of great antiquity' excavated at Jaffa (1887: 4), but the most detailed evidence relates to the coastline between Haifa and Akko. During a three-hour ride between these two ports Stephens (1838: 342-3) noted how 'The sea was calm, but the wrecks on the shore, of which we counted seventeen on our way to Caipha, told us that the elements of storm and tempest might lurk under a fair and beautiful face ...'. Stewart (1857: 452) also remarked on the abundant evidence of the inhospitable nature of the coast, counting eight wrecked vessels that had been driven onto shore a week before. Along the beaches of Akko, where the River Kishon enters the sea, Monro (1835: 56) observed how 'The entire shore round the bay is lashed by breakers, and the timbers which covered the sand bore ample testimony to its intensity as a harbour. At the eastern side were no less than ten wrecks in the course of a mile, three of which were Turkish ships of war of a small size.'

These comparative sources are particularly striking in their descriptions of rates of ship losses, and although scales of wreckage are related to the interaction between shipping levels, frequencies of storm episodes, their duration and ferocity, the application of these reports to different decades provides very strong evidence that shipwreck was a constant fear and reality. Today winter storm fronts cross Palestine every 6-10 days (Carmel *et al.* 1985: 1). Using Stewart's data above, and even by doubling the scientific evidence for storm frequency to one every 20 days, this suggests that winter storms (November to February inclusive) could result in localised wreckage rates

Shipwreck Archaeology

of a minimum of 48 ships. Applying this storm ratio to Monro's testimony results in a figure of 60 possible annual shipwrecks off Akko. Even by applying the highly conservative estimate that Stephens' 17 shipwrecks between Akko and Haifa, a distance of about 20 km, might have been lost over a 25-year period, one arrives at a minimum figure of 68 shipwrecks in this area for the nineteenth century alone. If we very conservatively estimate that, on average, a mere ten ships were wrecked off Palestine annually between 1200 BC and AD 1800, this results in a total wreckage figure of 30,000 loss events. With a booming economy and highly developed long-distance trade, it is not unrealistic to propose that some 3,200 ships were lost off the Holy Land between AD 320 and 640.

As incredible as these figures may sound, comparative global shipping figures demonstrate that these scales are far from unrealistic. In the 1860s 250 British ships annually were lost far out at sea. For the first millennium BC alone, more than 15,000 ships might have been lost in the Mediterranean and Black Seas (Bascom 1987: 222-3).

Obviously not every ship lost off the Holy Land contained a cargo, and not every cargo contained a form of commodity susceptible to preservation underwater. Without a heavy, durable metallic or ceramic cargo, or a veneer of stone ballast sealing a wooden hull, many ships would have been rapidly destroyed by a storm and washed onto shore. Wreckage rates will not equate to wreck detection rates in the archaeological record. Further, there is simply no means of assessing changes in shipping levels over time. Nevertheless, the data discussed does provide convincing new generalised ammunition to reject the notion that little of Israel's shipwreck heritage is left underwater. The argument that the 200 cargoes currently identified by the IAA represent the greater majority of the country's ancient shipwreck heritage is highly inaccurate and misleading. Certainly the ancient shipwreck heritage currently

2. Myths, misconceptions and maritime heritage

identified is but a drop in the ocean, unlikely to represent more than 20% of the total number of sites awaiting discovery off Israel today (excluding deep-water sites).

3
Site-formation analyses

Introduction

In the formative years of marine archaeology, unfamiliarity with shipwreck site-formations created unrealistic expectations of the type of shipwrecks present off the Israel coast. Reports of cargoes discovered by fishermen, and the experience gained during underwater surveys, have produced an elementary understanding of wreck preservation (Raban 1973), but detailed studies of the processes of wreckage, site sedimentation, post-disturbance by salvage and looting, and site erosion, have not been initiated. Yet without an understanding of these fundamental issues, regional levels of wreck preservation, the character of original cargoes, and the historical importance of wrecks will remain open to misinterpretation. Current levels of site-formation comprehension are currently well below the multi-dimensional reality.

Specific problems and inaccuracies examined in this chapter include:

(i) The pluralistic nature of surveys. Levels of site preservation and the presence of unusual artefacts are more likely to dictate survey methodology than the historical importance of a site.
(ii) Preservation theory reduces the integrity of survey. The misconception that ancient wrecks are essentially poorly preserved off Israel creates an excuse for simplistic sampling

3. Site-formation analyses

strategies that minimise initiatives to reconstruct original cargoes.

(iii) Misunderstanding of wreck site-formations results in skewed cultural resource management.

Shipwreck preservation and site-formation analysis

Shipwreck preservation and site-formation in Israel are dictated by the relationship between two geomorphological conditions. The first is the mild gradient of the continental shelf, which slopes westward mainly at an angle of one degree or less (Neev and Ben-Avraham 1977: 358). Rocky cliffs descending to depths of 20-30 m at the shoreline, prevalent off the coasts of southern France, Italy, Greece, Turkey and the Adriatic, are absent. Almost all of the 200 documented wrecks off Israel are located in shallow water between 1 and 6 m deep. Secondly, large quantities of Nile-derived sand transported along the coast by the anti-clockwise longshore gyre and wave motion comprise the dominant sedimentological feature overlying the seabed (Emery and Neev 1960: 4, 10). Sand accumulations exceeding heights of 3 m are common in shallow waters.

The shallow depth of most shipwrecks is not a consequence of limited survey parameters restricted to the near-shore zone, nor related to sea-level change, but is conditioned by the relationship between the region's coastal geomorphology and the prevalent storm climate. During adverse climatic conditions south-westerly winds and high waves forced ships toward the coast. Any vessel propelled shoreward, or attempting to beach herself deliberately, found controlled navigation difficult under these conditions and frequently grounded on submerged sandbanks – sometimes deliberately – or collided with offshore sandstone islets and the coastal ridge. The problem of ephemeral sandbanks is described by Josephus Flavius in relation to the harbours of Dor and Joppa, c. 22 BC (*Jewish Antiquities* XV.333; Marcus 1963: 161): 'the south-west wind beats on them and always dredges up sand from the sea upon the shore, and thus does not permit a smooth landing; instead it is usually necessary for merchants to ride unsteadily at anchor off shore'. The efficiency of sounding leads, normally employed to determine the depth of water between a keel and the seabed to facilitate safe navigation (Oleson 1988: 30-4), would have been limited during extreme storms when ship movement lay essentially in the lap of the gods.

Wooden ships that founder in depths exceeding about 20 m in the Mediterranean Sea tend to form well-preserved wreck sites (Parker 1984: 100) because disturbance by currents and wave motion is limited and salvage complicated by relatively difficult access. By contrast, ships wrecked off the coast of Israel were subjected to extreme post-depositional disturbance that does not favour good preservation of cargoes, although deep sand accumulations can preserve wooden hulls.

If sediments rapidly covered a wreck and its cargo before a storm abated, inaccessibility and the anaerobic conditions present within sand blankets could enable deposits to stabilise and be preserved. These conditions, however, assume minimal subsequent wreck exposure, and few examples of this site-formation are known in Israel. If accurate, Saewulf's description of 'ships dashed against each other and broken into small pieces' in the port of Jaffa in 1102 or 1103 (Clifton 1896: 6) lends credence to the plausibility that a wooden ship could break up rapidly in the course of a single storm. If an ancient ship was destroyed in this manner, its proximity to the shore and vulnerability to high-energy wave motion would have caused any ceramic cargo to quickly fragment. The only preserved traces of the original ship would be heavy metallic and stone objects deposited on the seabed. This model is considered the prevalent one for shipwreck site-formations off Israel (Misch-Brandl and Galili 1985: 11).

3. Site-formation analyses

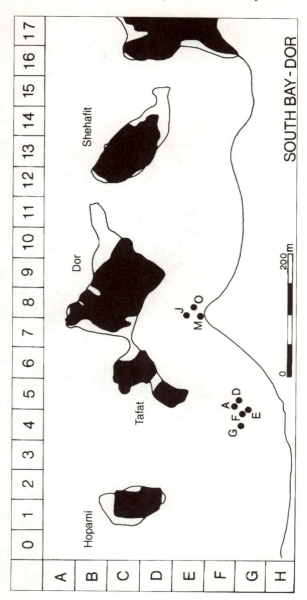

Fig. 3. Byzantine ships wrecked between the offshore islets and shore in the southern anchorage at Dor.

Shipwreck Archaeology

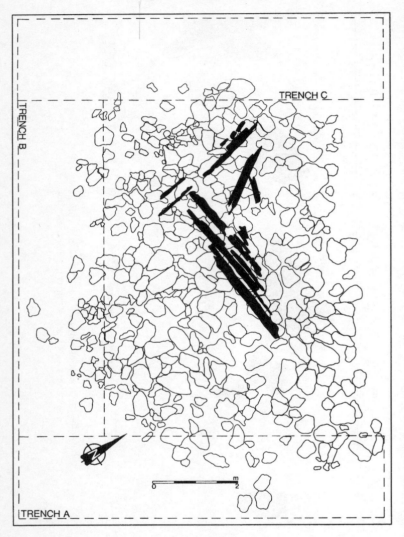

Fig. 4. Surface manifestations of the late sixth-century AD Dor D shipwreck with ballast overlying wooden planking (solid black).

3. Site-formation analyses

However, archaeological and comparative nineteenth-century sources clarify that shipwrecks must have been a common sight along Palestine's coastline throughout antiquity and the early modern period. They also clearly demonstrate that, in reality, the majority of wrecked ships deteriorated slowly, enabling their cargoes to be salvaged. A wreck in Haifa Bay featured prominently in a painting made by the artist David Roberts in 1839 (see the cover of this book). At the same coastal city, Tristram (1866: 95) observed 'the grim skeletons of many a coaster, driven high on shore, stripped of all but the main timbers, which still stood erect, in black groups here and there, the favourite perches of the osprey and the cormorant'. Descriptions of numerous wooden hulls along the shoreline between Haifa and Akko, described in Chapter 2, confirm that the unique geomorphology and coastal climate of Palestine resulted in shipwrecked hulls being common landmarks.

Although nineteenth-century wooden merchant vessels were almost certainly more robust than their ancient equivalents, because they relied on iron nails and bolts rather than wooden mortise-and-tenon joints for assembly, the discovery of ancient wooden hulls at Ma'agan Michael (c. 400 BC; Linder 1993), Caesarea (late first century BC; Fitzgerald 1994) and Dor (Byzantine, Abassid and post-medieval; Kingsley and Raveh 1996; Wachsmann *et al.* 1997; Figs 3-7) prove that ships frequently survived storms throughout antiquity. The duration that a wreck remained visible in the surf zone or on the edge of a beach, and its subsequent deterioration, depended fortuitously on the location where a ship foundered and the speed with which the hull was covered with sand or dismantled by local inhabitants for recycling or firewood.

The cargoes of ancient ships that were not destroyed during the course of a single storm could be relatively easily salvaged from shallow waters. Both ancient and early modern historical and comparative sources validate this theory. The Chevalier

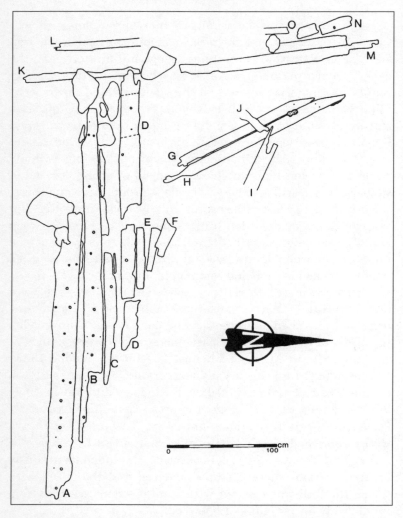

Fig. 5. Plan of scattered hull planking from the late sixth-century AD Dor D shipwreck.

3. Site-formation analyses

Fig. 6. Hull planking from the late sixth-century AD Dor D shipwreck.

d'Arvieux described the recovery of barrels of Cypriot wine and cheese from a Greek ship wrecked at Dor in 1664 (Labat 1717: 91-2). Stephens (1838: 354) observed a wrecked schooner at Rosh Hanniqra whose 'shivered sails [were] still flying from the masts, and the luckless mariners were alongside in a small boat, bringing ashore the remnant of the cargo'. Between Haifa and Akko, Stewart (1857: 452) observed how one of the eight wrecked vessels driven onto the shore was a French vessel whose 'crew had made a rude tent with one of the sails, and were endeavouring to save such portions of the cargo and spars as the heavy surf washed up'.

The pursuit of salvage in Late Antiquity as a financially lucrative activity is evident from a passage in the seventh-century AD Rhodian Sea-Law, which stipulated that where nautical material was raised from eight fathoms (about 15 m), the salvor received one-third of all objects retrieved. Wrecked objects cast from the sea onto land or found at a depth of one cubit (about 50 cm) entitled the finder to one-tenth of what was recovered (Ashburner 1909: 119). According to this law, cargoes submerged at depths of 1 to 6 m off Palestine would have entitled a salvage team to at least 10% of the value of the objects raised. The scarcity of amphorae encountered on wrecks along the Israel coast may be explained partly by the success of

Fig. 7. Plan of the sixth-century AD Tantura A hull from Dor (from Kahanov and Royal 1996: 21).

3. Site-formation analyses

salvage in antiquity: complete amphorae have only been reported from three Byzantine wrecks, the late fourth-century Carmel Beach A site (Raban 1969-71: 67-9; Fig. 27, no. 1), the early seventh-century AD Dor J ship (Kingsley 1994-5: 44) and off Neve Yam (Galili and Sharvit 1999: 100). If ship salvage was conducted, only pottery broken during the act of wreckage and wedged in crevices between stone ballast blocks, or material from the galley stored above the hold (which had drifted away from the wreck and had been concealed by sand), would have been preserved on most wrecks.

Shipwreck sampling strategies

Misunderstanding of shipwreck site-formations has resulted in somewhat arbitrary and data-damaging sampling strategies in Israel. Archaeologists have assumed that the hulls of almost all wrecks are poorly preserved and that scattered, fragmentary cargoes are incapable of reconstruction. In turn, such theory is used to excuse the prevailing random sampling strategies adopted during surveys and based on intuitive procurement. Consequently, sites' interpretative potential tend to be prejudged prior to survey, justifying grab sampling. Since no patterns can be extracted from scattered wrecks, why implement analytical sampling strategies?

However, the formations of far too few wrecks have been investigated and published to justify such assumptions, and case studies from Dor leave no doubt that even relatively poorly preserved ships can yield crucial primary data: intact rigging blocks, galley roof tiles and hearth bricks, fragments of cargo amphorae, and even ballast stones all have important trade related tales to impart if we are capable of defining the information sought.

Realities of site-formation on Israel's largely scattered and, at best, partly coherent wrecks actually demand far more analytical strategies, in particular total recovery of surviving cargo and domestic assemblage, to maximise a site's interpretation value. A significant sample of amphorae rims, handles, bases and sherds can enable the original cargo character and final itinerary of a ship to be reconstructed. Such analyses are common on poorly preserved, scattered shipwrecks in the western Mediterranean, even amongst 'marine cemeteries' where cargoes from different ships have smeared together (Parker 1979; 1981). So why are comparable studies so woefully limited in Israel, simply based on an assumption that this form of analytical sampling is meaningless? The excavation of the late sixth-century AD Dor D shipwreck (Figs 4-6), which implemented total sherd recovery (Kingsley 2002), has proven that intensive sampling can form the basis of historical interpretation (see Chapter 4).

Site-formation analysis remains very poorly developed when juxtaposed against the high level of fieldwork conducted, leaving ongoing and future shipwreck sampling susceptible to severe data loss and site misinterpretation. A major implication of the site-formation theory discussed above is that a far greater variety of sites and quantity of wooden hulls await discovery off Israel than is assumed currently. This point of clarity has great significance for long-term cultural resource management in relation to future coastal development.

4

The shipwrecks of Byzantine Palestine

Sample characterisation

In terms of basic interpretative potential, shipwreck archaeology ought to serve as a superlative tool for studying the impact of inter-regional trade in the economy of Byzantine Palestine. Depending on levels of preservation, shipwreck analyses can theoretically be used to reconstruct diverse socio-economic conditions:

- Cargoes indicate types and quantities of agricultural and industrial produce imported to and exported from a region.
- Cargo composition reflects whether a vessel was involved in commerce (open trade) or closed forms of exchange (state or church redistribution for creating and maintaining social or political alliances).
- Graffiti and painted *tituli picti* on cargo amphorae can provide insights into the social structure of manufacture and export (by the state, church or private individuals).
- Organic residues preserved within amphorae – highly rare on archaeological settlements – can verify contents.
- Pottery associated with well-dated shipwrecks offers excellent opportunities to refine mainstream ceramic typologies.
- A ship's homeland can be determined by examining the personal domestic wares used by crews and indicate what provinces controlled shipping.

Shipwreck Archaeology

- Wreck dimensions and hull construction methods can reflect shipping organisation (state-controlled or entrepreneur oriented).
- A representative sample of shipwrecks containing similar cargo attributes or hull construction features can enable a long-term history of regional trade and economy to be compiled.
- Rhythms of maritime trade can be investigated to objectively assess the impact of historically attested political and environmental events.

To what degree do the Byzantine shipwrecks recorded off Israel shed light on these ideals? In order to address this question, eight patterns currently identifiable amongst the shipwrecks of the Holy Land will be discussed through reference to 23 shipwrecks from ten different sites. Following a presentation of the primary data (summarised below), trade patterns and the parameters of interpretation are debated. The eight patterns perceived are:

(i) Cargoes of raw materials (intra-regional trade): stone architecture (mainly recycled from ancient coastal settlements); scrap metal cargoes; raw glass cullet. Typical cargoes: stone masonry, marble panels, columns and capitals; lead sheet; glass ingots.
(ii) Amphora cargoes (inter-regional wine export): LR4 vessels from the Ashkelon/Gaza region and LR5 vessels produced throughout Palestine.
(iii) Amphora cargoes (inter-regional semi-luxury foodstuff import): Keay I, HC1, LR1 and LR2 vessels.
(iv) Domestic assemblages used by ships' crews: pitchers, cooking-pots and lids of copper with crenellated seams; white marble mortars for food preparation; hearth brick and galley roof tiles. Turkish and Cypriot provenances.

4. The shipwrecks of Byzantine Palestine

Late antique shipwrecks recorded off Israel

Site	Date	Length (m)	Site/cargo	Reference
Ashkelon A	Byz	--	masonry, column drums	CMS News 1988
Atlit D	Late Byz	--	LR5 amphorae	Ronen & Olami 1978: 36
Atlit E	Late Byz	--	scrap metal	Ullmann & Galili 1994
Caesarea A	4th-7th c	--	LR4 amphorae	Raban 1992: 114
Caesarea B	4th-7th c	--	LR4 amphorae	Raban 1992: 114
Carmel Beach A	380-390	--	Keay I and HC1 amphorae	Raban 1969-71: 67-9
Carmel Beach B	4th c	--	--	Galili et al. 1993: 72
Dor A	c. 600-640	22 ?	ballast	Kingsley & Raveh 1996: 61-4
Dor D	c. 575-600	15	LR4, LR5	Kingsley 2002
Dor E	6th-7th c	--	ballast	Kingsley & Raveh 1996: 66-7
Dor F	c. 600-640	--	ballast, masonry	Kingsley & Raveh 1996: 67-9
Dor G	c. 600-640	9+	masonry	Kingsley & Raveh 1996: 69-72
Dor J/ Tantura A	415-530*	12	LR5 amphorae	Kahanov & Royal 1996
Dor N/ Tantura B	680-850*	19-30	hull	Wachsmann 1996
Dor O	553-645*	--	masonry, hull	Wachsmann & Kahanov 1997: 10
Dor M	6th c	13.5	hull	Mor 2002-2003
Ginosar B	Late Byz	--	hull	Steffy 1990: 42-4
Givat Olga	6th-7th c	--	ballast, LR4 amphorae	Edgerton et al. 1980: 23
Hahotrim C	Byz	--	masonry, capitals, columns	Wachsmann & Raveh 1985
Neve Yam B	Late Rom/Byz	--	--	Parker 1992a: 288
Sdot Yam C	5th-6th c	--	LR4 amphorae	Raban 1989: 234
Sdot Yam D	1st half 4th c	--	lead sheet, amphorae	Galili et al. 1993: 68
Sdot Yam E	Byz	--	marble bowls, columns	Galili et al. 1993: 68

* Radio-carbon date.

(v) Recycling of amphorae and iron anchors: economic decline or ideological preference?
(vi) Evidence for Christian shipping management.
(vii) Evidence of medium-level commerce.
(viii) Wooden hull remains and construction methods: evidence of middle-class merchants in shipping.

Shipwreck Archaeology

Intra-regional maritime trade

Throughout the Byzantine period the coastline of Palestine would have been teeming with local craft involved in low-level trade of minimal economic importance, and several shipwrecks provide a flavour of this activity. Cargoes of re-used stone masonry and architectural fragments in the form of rectangular ashlar blocks, each measuring 75 x 25 cm on average, have been recorded on three wrecks at Dor, dating between *c.* AD 600 and 640 (sites A, F and G; Kingsley and Raveh 1996: 61-2, 67, 69). Eroded and chipped surfaces and edges confirm that this material had already been used prior to shipment. Although the mixing of building masonry and amorphous boulders on two wrecks (Dor A and F) suggests use as ballast, other ships seem to have been involved specifically in the relocation of used masonry (Ashkelon A and Dor G).

Metal recycling was common in Palestine throughout antiquity, and evidence exists for merchants re-using stocks of lead and bronze in Late Antiquity. The Sdot Yam D cargo (south Caesarea) is associated with coins of Constantine and included 20 used and rolled lead sheets weighing 750 kg (Galili *et al.* 1993: 68). A wreck in the Main Bay at Dor of probable Late Roman or Early Byzantine date contains a lead cargo of folded scrap sheet, fishing-net weights and broken brail rings formerly used on ships' rigging (Kingsley and Raveh 1996: 55, pls 49-50). Part of a scrap-metal cargo of possible seventh-century date has been recorded in Atlit, including a Greek dedicatory inscription on a bronze plaque referring to the town of Sycamina (Fig. 8). A Jewish *menorah* is inscribed on the plaque, which may have originated from the synagogue of this coastal site, located in modern Haifa (Ullmann and Galili 1994: 116, 120-1).

The implications of amorphous glass ingots found scattered along the Carmel coast in the anchorage of Apollonia (Grossmann 1995: 160) and off Tell Hreiz (Galili and Sharvit 1999: 98)

4. The shipwrecks of Byzantine Palestine

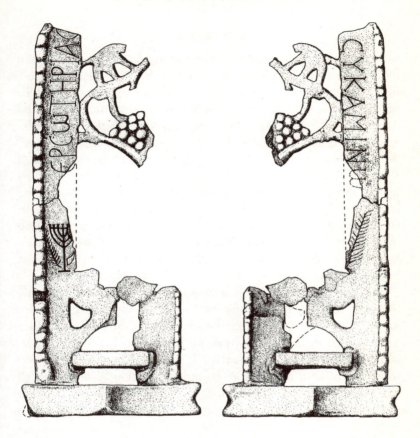

Fig. 8. Decorative bronze synagogue plaque from a seventh-century AD cargo in Atlit bay (from Ullmann and Galili 1994: 121).

confirm that cullet was transported over considerable distances as a commodity in its own right. But like scrap-metal cargoes, no indications are available about the size of these consignments or, indeed, about the ships that carried them. Were they undergoing transport for regional or long-distance trade? (See below and Chapter 5.)

Amphora cargoes

Seven wrecks containing amphora cargoes have been published from Israel, but provide a marginal view of the original scale and variety of products available at the time. Although 38 types of imports from North Africa, Egypt, Syria, Cyprus, Turkey, the Aegean and Spain have been recorded on Byzantine settlements in Israel (Kingsley 1999a: 164), this extensive import network is only reflected by a single ship off Israel. Carmel Beach A is a poorly preserved, scattered wreck, dated by coins to the decade AD 380-90 (Raban 1969-71: 67-9). The cargo contained Keay I oil amphorae from Mauretania and rare, thick-walled HC1 wine containers of possible Syrian origin (Fig. 27, nos 1 and 3). The presence on one ship of two amphora types produced in distant geographical regions suggests that both may have been procured at a single entrepot.

Four cargoes of tall, cylindrical LR4 wine amphorae originating from the Gaza and Ashkelon region (Israel 1995; Johnson and Stager 1995: 99-100) have been recorded at Caesarea, Sdot Yam and Givat Olga (see Table on p. 47; Fig. 21). LR4 sherds, some lined with pitch indicative of a wine content, are known from two wrecks dated to c. AD 600-40 at Dor (sites A and E: Kingsley and Raveh 1996: 64, 67). Poor preservation has prevented determining the original quantity of amphorae transported on these ships and whether this material comprised cargo or domestic assemblage. However, quantification of the fragmented cargo amphorae excavated from the late sixth-century Dor D ship suggested that the LR4 component represented 7% of the total cargo (Kingsley 2002: 26).

A late sixth-/early seventh-century site at Givat Olga is particularly interesting because it was identified at a depth of 40 m by side-scan sonar (Edgerton *et al.* 1980: 7, 13) and is located along an international sea-lane north of the region whence the cargo originated. It is unlikely that this ship would

4. The shipwrecks of Byzantine Palestine

have tacked so far offshore if the LR4 cargo had been intended for intra-regional trade within Palestine. The quantity of amphora fragments associated with this site is unpublished.

Bag-shaped LR5 wine amphorae manufactured in central and southern Palestine (Kingsley 1994-5; Fig. 21) have been recorded on seven Byzantine wrecks in Israel, located within the southern anchorage at Dor and Atlit harbour (Dor A, D, E, F, G and J: Kingsley and Raveh 1996: 61-9; Atlit D: Ronen and Olami 1978: 36). All examples from Dor were pitch-lined, indicative of wine content. Limited sampling strategies once again complicate our interpretation of this material as cargo or containers from the ship's galley stores, although the non-Palestinian character of some material culture from domestic assemblages on these sites is a strong indication that the LR4 and LR5 amphorae were cargo destined for inter-regional transport. Quantification conducted on southern Palestinian LR5 amphorae associated with the late sixth-century Dor D wreck interpreted the 668 rims, bases, handles and sherds as a primary cargo (89% of all amphorae; Fig. 2). One LR5 sherd recovered from the ship still had grape-pips embedded within pitch lining the interior of its wall (Kingsley 2002: 34), confirming for the first time a definite association between LR5 amphorae and wine. Notably, this evidence was only detected by implementing a programme of total sherd recovery on this only partly coherent site with a scattered cargo. A second, better preserved cargo of stylistically diverse LR5 amphorae is associated with Dor J (Kingsley 1994-5; Sibella 1995a). Radiocarbon analysis of hull timbers dates the site to between AD 415 and 530 (Carmi and Segal 1995: 12).

Although limited publication and simplistic sampling complicate interpretation of these LR4 and LR5 cargoes, the volume of deposits recorded suggests that export of these wine jars was a primary economic activity in Byzantine Palestine. Dor D's domestic assemblage and its 346 amorphous ballast stones (Fig. 4) suggest that this vessel was incoming from western Cyprus. (The 'cargo' seems to have comprised empty amphorae destined for recycling; Kingsley 2002: 11, 15, 26-7; see below.) This export pattern is confirmed by cargoes of Palestinian amphorae recorded off southern Turkey at Kizilagac Adasi and Kekova Oludeniz, on an important sixth- or early seventh-century shipwreck at Iskandil Burnu (306 amphorae: Lloyd 1984: 61, n. 44), and at La Palud, Port Cros, off southern France, on a wreck of the middle or second half of the sixth century (Long and Volpe 1998: 337, 339). A complete bag-shaped amphora of fourth- to fifth-century date found off Corfu must also have originated from a wreck site (personal communication, D. Kourkoumelis, 1998). Individual Palestinian amphorae have also been recorded in anchorages at Serçe Liman in Turkey (Lloyd 1984: n. 44), and off Cyprus at Cape Andreas, Hala Sultan Tekke (McCaslin 1978: figs 225-6) and Keratidhi Bay (Morris and Peatfield 1987: fig. 2, no. 045).

Domestic assemblages

Since most cargoes on ancient shipwrecks were composite in character, assembled at different ports or in a single entrepot (Parker 1990: 343), identifying the homeland of a ship and crew often offers different interpretative permutations. Domestic assemblages theoretically contain the most revealing categories of artefacts capable of verifying provenance. This assumes that crews predominantly chose to be culturally affiliated with domestic pottery and utensils manufactured in their homeland. Domestic assemblage can be defined as artefactual material within a ship's structure consisting of objects and foodstuffs essential for the daily livelihood of a small crew, and the personal belongings of the mariners and passengers (Gibbins 1989: 5). This class usually includes weighing apparatus and a carpenter's chest (Fig. 9).

4. The shipwrecks of Byzantine Palestine

Fig. 9. A pickaxe and hammer head and from wrecks Dor D and F respectively. Note the fine preservation of iron and some wooden shaft.

Fig. 10. Copper flask and cooking-pot from the wrecks Dor A and Dor G; AD 600-40. Note crenellated seams along bases.

Shipwreck Archaeology

Most domestic assemblages recorded on ancient shipwrecks tend to be concentrated in and around vestiges of a galley toward a ship's stern. Bricks and roof-tiles recorded on three Byzantine wrecks in Dor harbour (sites Dor A, D, F in Kingsley and Raveh 1996) originate from this feature. Material recorded on four Byzantine wrecks at Dor includes three flasks, two cooking-pots and a lid, each composed of one or more sheets of copper dove-tailed together at crenellated seams (Fig. 10). This feature typifies Late Byzantine north-eastern Mediterranean metallurgy, and all known examples are currently dated to the first half of the seventh century. Comparable artefacts from Turkey have been excavated on the Yassi Ada wreck (Katsev 1982: 269-70) and shops at Sardis operable until at least $c.$ AD 615/16 (Stephens Crawford 1990: 54, 94, figs 213-14, 522). No parallels to these utensils are known from the 2,930 Byzantine sites recorded on land in Israel.

A comparable provenance is likely for a white marble mortar from Dor A (Kingsley and Raveh 1996: 62, fig. 42) decorated with three semi-circular lugs on the outer rim edge and a false spout (Fig. 11). Early seventh-century typological comparisons from Turkey include an example from the Yassi Ada A wreck (Katsev 1982: 289) and from the church at Saraçhane (Gill 1986: 234). An exact parallel excavated in shop E9 at Sardis was probably deposited $c.$ AD 615/16 (Stephens Crawford 1990: 73, fig. 333).

Further evidence for a north-eastern Mediterranean origin for merchant vessels operating off Palestine in Late Antiquity is provided by an unpublished Cypriot Red Slip Form 9 bowl found on wreck Dor E, and by the late sixth-century Dor D shipwreck. The 346 ballast blocks from this ship (Fig. 4) have been provenanced to the Cypriot regions of the Troodos massif and Ayia Varvara, Paphos (Kingsley 2002: 15). Petrological analyses conducted on LR1 amphorae and roof-tiles from this ship's domestic assemblage also reflect a Cypriot origin (Wil-

4. The shipwrecks of Byzantine Palestine

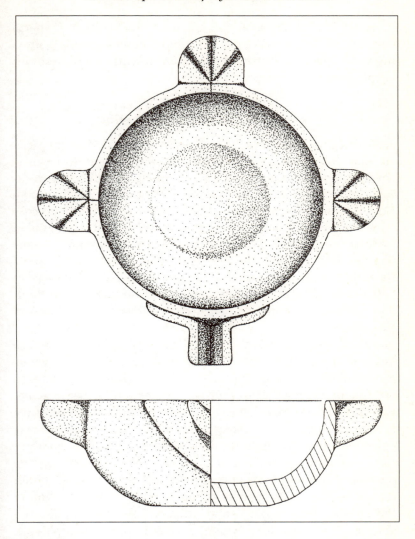

Fig. 11. White marble mortar from wreck Dor A; AD 600-40. Width: 35 cm (drawing: D. Avni).

liams 2002: 111). The available evidence thus strongly supports origins in Turkey and Cyprus for the merchant vessels operating in Dor harbour during the later sixth century and first half of the seventh century.

Amphora and anchor recycling

A crucial historical question in Late Antique studies concerns the date when 'Classical' Antiquity drew to an end. As regards the western Mediterranean this heavyweight intellectual question has spawned huge debate, but of the eastern basin discussion is surprisingly sparse. Was decline a gradual process triggered by the Justinianic plague of AD 541 and compounded by further environmental catastrophes, including earthquakes and harvest failure? Did the Arab Conquest of AD 640 irreparably dislocate trade networks or did the Umayyad dynasty deliberately continue Byzantine forms of administration? Well-dated shipwrecks ought to clarify the economic dimension of this debate.

Shipwrecks dated to the critical time spanning c. AD 550 to 640 and involved in long-distance trade in Palestinian wines are conspicuous within Dor harbour (see Table on p. 47), but are not free of complex interpretative problems. For instance, between c. AD 400 and at least the end of the seventh century Byzantine anchors were composed of iron, with straight arms positioned at right angles to the shank in a cruciform configuration (Joncheray 1975: 119-20; van Doorninck 1982b). The cruciform Byzantine anchor was the standard type off Israel and examples have been recorded in the harbour of Iamnia Paralios, modern Yavne Yam (Galili *et al.* 1993: 63), and in the anchorage of Apollonia (Grossman 1995: 174). Six examples are known immediately north of the port of Caesarea (Raban 1989: 231), and 19 anchors have been examined in Dor harbour (Kingsley and Raveh 1996: 21).

4. The shipwrecks of Byzantine Palestine

Fig. 12. Arms and lower shanks of encrusted Byzantine iron anchors from wreck Dor J, before conservation.

The early seventh-century Dor J wreck is associated with four anchors (Fig. 12), all curiously broken along the shank and in two instances with the arms no longer intact (Kingsley and Raveh 1996: pl. 57). Following snagging on reefs and subsequent salvage, this anchor group seems to have been retained with the intention of repair. Reconstituting anchors was facilitated by the tendency to weld them together from several sections of iron. Individual anchors from the eleventh-century Serçe Limani wreck were composed of as many as 15 sections of iron (van Doorninck 1988: 25). Evidence that a fluke on an anchor from the Yassi Ada A ship of *c*. AD 625/6 had been filed down and reshaped after breaking (Haldane 1985: 7) suggests that comparable care was taken in the Byzantine period to prolong an anchor's life.

A further complication off Israel is the unusual association of one-hole stone anchors, very much the poor man's substitute, with three sixth- and early seventh-century shipwrecks (Kingsley and Raveh 1994). Anchors were essentially ships' umbilical cords, and no sea captain concerned with the welfare of his vessel and cargo could afford to rely on inferior breaking mechanisms. Is this evidence of economic decline preceding the Arab invasion of Palestine?

A second dimension to the argument is amphora recyling. The LR5 bag-shaped cargo amphorae from Dor J seem to have been produced in various potters' workshops and display evidence of re-use. Dated quite widely between c. 550 and 660, they exhibit diverse clay fabrics and shapes (Raveh and Kingsley 1991: 203; Kingsley 1994-5: 44), and while some have straight sides, the majority are round with a curved shoulder, waist and base. Some are decorated with white-painted straight and curvilinear horizontal and vertical lines; others are plain. Rims are all very short (2-3 cm high), but several subtle variants have been recorded: collared, straight and convex. Two fabrics occur, dark grey and light reddish-brown. The combination of form and fabric suggests that these amphorae derived from several different kilns. Although pitch lining the inner amphora surfaces of this cargo is indicative of an original wine content, the rims of three were damaged prior to shipment when the jars' stoppers were prised open, and an olive-pit was embedded in the resinous lining of another container, although fig and grape seeds in its base seem to be remains of former contents (Sibella 1995a: 15).

Similar stylistic and clay fabric variation has been recorded on the late sixth-century Dor D ship, most notably amongst the LR5 amphorae. In addition to three distinct rim profiles, five clay fabrics have been identified, indicative of manufacture in different sources and workshops. The vent hole of one amphora (used to release carbon dioxide build-up in this specific type of wine jar) was sealed with a lead plug, certain evidence of re-use (Kingsley 2002: 85).

4. The shipwrecks of Byzantine Palestine

Shipping management: religious contexts

The question of the extent to which religious orders managed aspects of shipping in Late Antiquity has currently received little archaeological attention. Cargo amphorae on board the Yassi Ada A ship wrecked off Turkey *c.* AD 625/6 may have been procured from ecclesiastical estates, and the Greek inscriptions on the ship's steelyard points to church control of this vessel (van Alfen 1996).

The limited evidence available from Israel unsurprisingly reflects strong Christian involvement in sea trade. Steelyards were an essential means of verifying the weight of merchandise and are common on merchant vessels from the first century onwards. Two bronze steelyards, suspension chains and a lead counterweight sheathed in copper are associated with Dor G, wrecked between *c.* AD 600 and 640 (Kingsley and Raveh 1996: 69-72). The steelyards are 11 cm and 97 cm long and inscribed with Greek calibration marks along the beam, which register up to just under 160 pounds. Using a conversion rate of one Byzantine pound to a maximum of 318.5 grams (Sams 1982: 229), the large steelyard could record a maximum weight of about 51 kg, sufficient to weigh one full amphora amongst the cargo.

The terminals of both balances bear Greek inscriptions bordered by Christian crosses (Fig. 13). One of three inscriptions on the large steelyard is repeated on the smaller example and indicates that at the date of wreckage the pair's owner was a merchant called Psates of Rhion (de la Presle 1993: 581, 585). According to the formula of this text, this individual was Christian. Two additional inscriptions on other edges of the larger device refer to two former owners, also Christian. One has been translated as 'Jesus Christ, come to the aid of George (son) of Ision', and the other more tentatively as 'Saviour Jesus Christ, come to the aid of Khala .../ and Artemon' (de la Presle 1993:

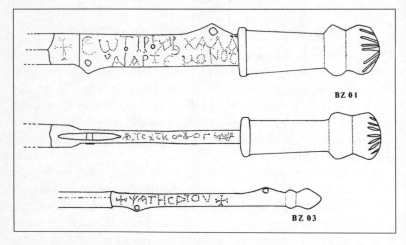

Fig. 13. Greek inscriptions on the collars of two steelyards from wreck Dor G; AD 600-40.

582-3). The presence of three inscriptions on one steelyard suggests longevity of use, evidence of the object's coveted role in trade transactions.

A Greek cross incised into the hull of the Dor O ship (Wachsmann and Kahanov 1997: 10) probably hints at little else than construction by a Christian shipwright. More interesting is a Byzantine wreck surveyed off Hahotrim containing a cargo of ashlar masonry, marble capitals and columns decorated with crosses (Wachsmann and Raveh 1985: 37). The preliminary impression of this site (based on highly limited published details) is of a ship possibly transporting prefabricated architectural fragments intended for the construction of a church, similar to the sixth-century Marzamemi B vessel off Sicily (Kapitän 1969). Such a hypothesis is not unrealistic: imported Proconnesian marble has been identified at many sites in *Palaestina Tertia* (Sodini 1989: 184). However, in the absence of a detailed report about the worked condition of the marble and the specific forms of architecture represented, the

4. The shipwrecks of Byzantine Palestine

possibility that this cargo comprises *spolia* removed from a coastal city for recycling cannot be excluded. Other evidence for comparable marble cargoes includes a marble column (Proconnesian?), base and unused marble slabs associated with the Tantura A wreck, possibly intended for the Christian basilica at Dor (Sibella 1995b: 19-20).

Unequivocal evidence of Jewish operatives in maritime trade is absent from the shipwreck sources (although historical texts and imported pottery confirm their involvement; see Chapters 5-6). A curious possible exception are bag-shaped LR5 amphorae which incorporate a small, circular vent hole about one cm in diameter, cut into the shoulder, found in ancient harbours all along the coast of Israel. This attribute is extremely unusual and does not occur among the repertoire of well-known Roman types of amphorae or among contemporary Byzantine forms. Two possible interpretations are likely. Had international demand for Holy Land wines reached such high levels that amphorae were being filled with immature produce still fermenting, relying on vent holes to release continuing carbon dioxide build-up? Very possibly, given the evidence for extensive quantities exported as far as the western Mediterranean (see Chapter 6). Or was the vent hole an attribute of Jewish viticulture, invented to maintain standards of ritual purity (*halakhah*) demanded by Jewish consumers? Given that vent holes have been recorded on second- and third-century AD Palestinian amphorae, suggesting a prolonged tradition, the latter interpretation seems more logical.

Shipping management: social contexts

Late Antiquity is envisaged by both historians and archaeologists as a period of major social transformation in the organisation of long-distance maritime trade. The Byzantine state's control over the distribution of *annona civica* (natural tax in kind procured from the provinces distributed as dole to Constantinople and other major cities) and over industrial production, such as purple dye processing and its shipment, is believed to have broken down. A decline in the average size of merchant vessels and a radical change in ship construction methodology are considered non-coincidental and to reflect a 'revolution' in the structure of maritime trade, whereby middle-class merchants became increasingly prevalent.

By the late fourth century historical sources hint at cracks in state interests. Illegal activities discussed in the Theodosian Code include attempts to avoid compulsory public shipment by registering a ship under the name of a second party, and shipmasters bribing dignitaries or officials responsible for *annona* grain shipment. Such corruption presumably enabled a shipmaster to profit by transporting a commercial cargo alongside a state consignment. Thus an edict of AD 395 (*CTh*. 13.8.1; Pharr 1952: 399) ruled that '[no] person shall place a private burden upon a public cargo, nor shall he dare to compel, by any necessity, the carriers of grain to accept his burden'.

An increased importance of small merchant vessels is argued by Lopez (1959: 71) to have been a consequence of the disappearance of state transportation and the increasingly hostile Islamic presence in the eastern Mediterranean in the Late Byzantine period, which forced sailors to adapt nautical technology to changing economic and political conditions. A new type of steering-oar was developed, use of the lateen sail was standardised, and references to new ship types (such as the *gazelle*) suggested a preference for smaller, more agile craft. Cheaper to build, easier to maintain, and financially a smaller investment and risk to own than large vessels, small ships were 'a powerful factor of democracy' because they suited the limited income bracket of many sailors and merchants (Lopez 1959: 79).

Evidence for the privatisation of long-distance trade has

4. The shipwrecks of Byzantine Palestine

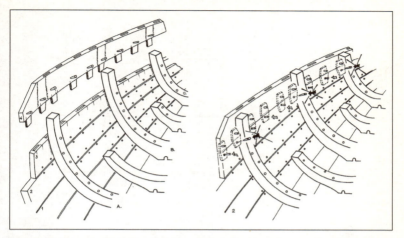

Fig. 14. Schematic drawing of a side section of a second-century AD Roman hull. Note how outer strakes are attached by inserting tenons into mortises (left) and how these are locked in place using wooden treenails (right) (after Cuomo and Gassend 1982: 265).

been posited by marine archaeologists in the transition from classical tenon-built ships to frame-first technology in Late Antique shipwrecks. Most ancient wooden merchant vessels until the Early Byzantine period were constructed using a 1,700-year-old technology known as 'shell first' or 'tenon-built' shipbuilding. After the keel and end-posts were erected, the strakes (outer planking) were connected using mortise-and-tenon fastenings set on both edges of a strake and locked in place using wooden pegs (Fig. 14). The insertion of the internal skeletal infrastructure inside the hull, including the frames, was a secondary process implemented only after a complete section of the external planking was intact. Closely and evenly spaced mortise-and-tenon joints produced enormous longitudinal strength (Steffy 1995: 22). Although diverse construction techniques co-existed throughout antiquity on tenon-built ships, including the insertion of some frames before the completion of upper sections of external planking ('construction

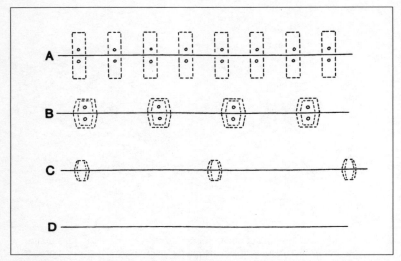

Fig. 15. Schematic drawing illustrating the general change in mortise-and-tenon ship joinery between the late fourth century BC (A), the fourth century AD (B), the seventh century AD (C), and the ninth century AD (D) (from Steffy 1994: 84).

alternée' in Cuomo and Gassend 1982; Pomey 1994: 126), and the use of rope ligatures to sew planks together (Lehmann 1991: 24), all are characterised by a primary concentration on the external planking to provide the vessel's fundamental structural strength.

During the Roman period, square or rectangular mortises were cut deeply into underlying and overlying strakes and spaced about 10-12 cm apart on average (Steffy 1994: 37-78; Fig. 14). As many as 20,000 mortise-and-tenon joints might be required to build a large Roman freighter (Steffy 1995: 421). However, a radically new methodology evolved between the fourth and seventh centuries (Fig. 15). By the late fourth century less attention was paid to these joints, which became smaller and more widely spaced. Thus, mortise-and-tenons on Dramont F, wrecked off southern France c. AD 400, were positioned between 19 and 36 cm apart (Joncheray 1975: 126). A

4. The shipwrecks of Byzantine Palestine

similar pattern has been recorded on the Dramont E wreck again off southern France, where distances between joints ranged between 10-14 cm in weak areas subjected to extreme stress, but 26-31 cm apart elsewhere. The latest coin dates this wreck to AD 425-55 or soon after (Santamaria 1995: 114, 144, 179).

A second stage in the transition from 'tenon-built' ships toward 'frame-first' vessels (skeleton construction) had been realised by the first half of the seventh century. On wrecks excavated at Pantano Longarini off Sicily (Throckmorton and Throckmorton 1973: 263), Yassi Ada A off southern Turkey (van Doorninck 1982a: 55) and St Gervais B off southern France (Jézégou 1989), mortises were no longer locked into tenons with wooden pegs, but were left loosely fitted (Fig. 15C). These joints now merely served to align the outer planks on top of one another until they were nailed to the inner frames, which now provided the main structural integrity. On the hull of St Gervais B, dated to the first quarter of the seventh century or slightly later, joints were only found at intervals exceeding 1 m in the lower extremities of the hull. The absence of mortise-and-tenon joints between the keel and garboard (lowest line of outer planking) indicates that some frames must have been attached to the keel before the strakes (Jézégou 1989: 140-1).

Ships built using mortise-and-tenons are labour-intensive and wasteful of wood (Steffy 1991: 1). The reduction in the number of mortise-and-tenon joints used on Byzantine merchant vessels, and the greater dependence on frames for internal strength, enabled ships to be built more cheaply and quickly (Hocker 1995: 203-4). Simultaneously, capital costs were reduced further by the abandonment of lead hull sheathing, previously used to protect joints and seams between outer planks and prevent marine fouling (Hocker 1995: 202). The latest dated ships externally sheathed in lead are the early fourth-century Femmina Morta hull, off Italy (Parker 1992a:

Fig. 16. Wooden hull planking among ballast stones from wreck Dor D, with an unpegged tenon protruding from its mortise; sixth century AD.

177), Grand Bassin D off southern France, dated to AD 313 (Solier 1981), and the early fourth-century Héliopolis A, also off southern France (Joncheray 1997: 158). Once abandoned, lead sealing was replaced by cheaper caulking methods (organic matter wedged between planks and sealed with pitch).

Analyses of shipwrecks off Israel have resulted in an important reassessment of the date of this Byzantine 'nautical revolution'. Wooden planking associated with wrecks Dor A and D revealed that both hulls were built using widely set mortise-and-tenons (Fig. 16), fitting into the traditional view of a gradual transition in Late Antiquity towards shell-first ships. Joints on the late sixth century Dor D ship were spaced between 17 and 44 cm apart and lacked locked wooden pegs (Kingsley 2002: 19). Two planks recorded between ballast on Dor A, dating between c. AD 600 and 640, utilised comparable technology (Kingsley and Raveh 1996: 62).

Although apparently earlier than both of these ships, the

4. The shipwrecks of Byzantine Palestine

hull of Tantura A wrecked off Dor, radio-carbon dated to between AD 415 and 530 (Carmi and Segal 1995: 12), was constructed in a completely different way (Fig. 7). No mortise-and-tenon joints occur on any planking or along the keel (Kahanov and Royal 1996: 22-3; Wachsmann and Kahanov 1997: 5). All the outer planking was nailed directly to the frames (inner reinforcement timbers) and iron nails fastened the frames to the keel. She was also in poor condition: the midship had been repaired using two narrow strips of planking, and the wide difference in dimensions and wood types used in the framing suggest to the reconstructors that the shipowner was an independent operator who was not wealthy (Kahanov and Royal 1996: 22). Tantura A is thus the earliest known example constructed using the frame-first skeletal technique. Preliminary analysis of the wreck Dor O, radio-carbon dated to AD 553-645, also failed to detect mortise-and-tenons (Wachsmann 1996: 19-20) and is indicative of a similar construction conception. The recent discovery of a third wreck in Dor of sixth-century date, also completely lacking mortise and tenon joints (Mor 2002-3), strengthens the argument that Holy Land commerce lay very much at the epicentre of this nautical adaptation. Before these discoveries the ninth-century Bozburun shipwreck had been considered the earliest known Mediterranean vessel built using frame-first technology (Hocker and Scafuri 1996: 8).

Conclusion

The preceding summary of the Byzantine shipwrecks of Israel clearly demonstrates that interpretation must be approached cautiously. Serious qualitative biases exist within the data. One is geographical. Except for Ginosar B, a fragment of a Late Byzantine vessel inadvertently uncovered in the Sea of Galilee (Steffy 1990: 42-4), and Ashkelon A (CMS News 1988), the remaining wrecks are all clustered between modern Tel Aviv and Haifa. Thirteen lie off Caesarea (including Sdot Yam) and Dor (see Table on p. 47).

This distribution cluster is an artificial pattern related to the volume of sediment deposited off the coast of Israel, which decreases according to distance away from the source at the Nile Delta in Egypt. While 400,000 m^3 of sand is conveyed annually to Gaza, only 80,000 m^3 reaches Atlit toward the north of Israel (Carmel *et al.* 1984: 1287). By contrast, the relative stability of submerged sand accumulations in southern Israel has obstructed wreck discovery in this area. Identification tends to be triggered by human interference in the form of coastal development. Surely to argue that the available sample is entirely representative of all Palestinian maritime trade in Late Antiquity would be stretching reality in improbable directions. Different agricultural and industrial activities must have been pursued in different cities, resulting in a shipment diversity that is currently simply not visible.

A second and more damaging bias is the quality of the data available. Survey is the prevailing methodological tool utilised off Israel, enabling maritime archaeological deposits temporarily exposed beneath sand blankets following winter storms to be recorded rapidly before shifting sediments re-conceal sites. Complete shipwreck concentrations are rarely entirely exposed naturally, resulting in a disproportionate appreciation of site value on the assumption that scattered sites retain limited interpretative value, thus excusing 'grab' sampling. A major problem concerns loss of data due to casual pottery procurement. More analytical studies based on total sherd recovery and quantification (counting or weighing each class of container) are essential if shipwreck archaeology off Israel is to achieve its potential. Because intact cargoes are simply unavailable, sampling must be tailored to maximise the data obtainable. Interpretation is further heavily compounded by the extremely

4. The shipwrecks of Byzantine Palestine

low and limited publication levels of dozens of shipwreck surveys conducted by IAA archaeologists. Consequently, we are mainly reliant on university and institutional research results.

Despite these limitations, several revealing patterns contribute important new information to studies of maritime trade in the Late Antique economy. Among the evidence for intra-regional trade, it is only glass ingot cargoes that would have been significant to the mainstream economy. But in the absence of contextual data from shipwrecks it is simply impossible to determine scales of production and export destinations, let alone specific dates for this industry. Should we envisage a comparable reality to the Serçe Limani ship, wrecked off Turkey c. 1025 with three tons of cullet (van Doorninck 1982c) and destined for overseas markets?

Shipwrecks containing both LR4 and LR5 amphorae indicate that wine was exported from Palestine over long distances in Late Antiquity. But precious little information exists from shipwrecks about scales of export, which provincial types comprised primary cargoes, what were their specific origins inside Palestine, and how the rhythms of the wine trade ebbed and flowed over time. Our information void would be vastly improved by the widespread adoption of standardised quantitative pottery analyses, as conducted on the sixth-century Dor D wreck (Kingsley 2002). More positively, broad evidence for wrecks dated c. AD 600-40 importantly demonstrates that long-distance trade continued after the Justinianic plague of AD 541 and up to the Arab Conquest of AD 640. Although a cargoless Abbasid-period wreck has been excavated at Dor (Wachsmann *et al.* 1997), no Umayyad wrecks and negligible harbour deposits post-dating the mid-seventh century have been recorded off Israel.

In contrast to the West Mediterranean, no evidence for North African pottery cargoes has been recorded off Israel (other than very limited evidence from the wreck Carmel Beach A). This is hardly surprising given the different trade orbits that existed between the East and West Mediterranean. But more problematic is how to explain the absence of Egyptian ships off Israel (and, indeed throughout the East Mediterranean) given the central role of Egyptian grain in the supply of *annona civica* to Constantinople. Historical evidence graphically describes how vast quantities of grain were shipped annually to Constantinople (Teall 1959). In the West, North African merchants rapidly exploited the state's established shipping infrastructure to fill the sea-lanes with oil, fish sauce, African Red Slip bowls and oil-lamps, and other products that are not preserved within the archaeological record. Adopting a similar economic model, why do we not see comparable exports along the Egypt/Constantinople export spine? The jury is currently out, although the huge quantities of Palestinian and Cypriot/Syrian amphorae excavated inside Egypt (Kingsley and Decker 2001: 4-5) are indicative of very healthy long-distance trade at least in one direction.

A similar dichotomy exists between extensive historical evidence for widespread tied exchange pursued by both Byzantine state and church (Monks 1953; Whittaker 1983: 167-70; Mundell Mango 2001), as well as by Jewish merchants and sailors (Fitzgerald 1926: 80-7; Sperber 1986), and an absence of shipwrecks. Is this situation explained by a diverse ship typology in Late Antiquity, with the high-level capital invested in state and church ships making their vessels better built and more robust than privately owned merchant vessels, thus reducing risks of wreckage? One would assume that the church cargoes of fabric, silver, silver litters, camels, birds, papyri and other luxury products transported on the squadron of ships from the likes of the see of St Mark in Alexandria (Monks 1953: 356; Mundell Mango 2001: 98-9), capable of carrying up to 20,000 *modii* (at least 128 tons), would have been crafted with more care than a merchant's amphora-bearing ship. Or is the absence of such vessels explained by their tendency to utilise sea-lanes located

4. The shipwrecks of Byzantine Palestine

far offshore, beyond depths currently explored by archaeological survey? Both explanations are unsatisfactory. As comparative sources discussed in Chapters 2-3 explained, the combination of geomorphology and storm climate forced troubled ships off Israel shoreward, where they generally ended up beached or foundering in the breaker zone. The probable answer is that this absence is due to both the infancy of the discipline and possibly unfamiliarity with forms of shipping in Late Antiquity, which may have resulted in incorrect site identification.

The domestic assemblages introduce original evidence for the involvement of Cypriot and Turkish merchants in the Palestinian wine trade. But our evidence only relates to the later sixth and first half of the seventh century and only to one type of cargo. Did a similar situation prevail in the fourth and fifth centuries and also for other types of shipments (metals, fineware pottery, foodstuffs)? While the two steelyards from the Dor G shipwreck demonstrate shipping control by Christian merchants, this is hardly a missing link for a church cargo.

The most complicated pattern visible among Byzantine shipwrecks off Israel is the recycling of amphorae and anchors. Although the retention of broken iron anchors can be explained away simply as due diligence, certainly the use of stone anchors superficially looks like either economic decline or low-level trade. But the stone examples occur on ships whose domestic assemblages are directly linked to Cyprus and Turkey, indicating that the vessels involved were capable of long-distance trade. However, both Dor D and Dor J contained empty Palestinian amphorae among their cargoes, apparently being shipped home for re-use. The shipmasters and merchants operating and financing these ships were clearly taking exceptional measures to maintain their investment. How can such a paradox be explained?

The overall impression is that several shipmasters passing

Shipwreck Archaeology

through Dor were experiencing economic hardship, which prevented them maintaining accepted standards for seafaring and trade. Multiple inscriptions from subsequent owners on Byzantine steelyards are uncommon (Ross 1962: 61-4; Garbsch 1988: 216-21), suggesting that the Dor G example had been in circulation for a long time and had been owned and sold by two former retired or deceased merchants before it was finally lost at sea. At present, the results from Dor seem to reflect widespread disruption of the eastern Mediterranean economy between the second half of the sixth and the first half of the seventh century. However, without doubt this is a highly misleading picture based on an overtly limited sample. As we shall discuss in Chapter 5, quantified amphora deposits excavated throughout the western Mediterranean, as well as extensive fine-wares imported into Palestine (see Chapter 6), prove that maritime trade remained healthy until the mid-seventh century.

Given this body of qualitatively superior evidence, the pattern derived from shipwrecks off Israel suggests very little more than the existence of a broad hierarchy of shipping functions in Late Antiquity. The Dor merchant vessels are very different to the Iskandil Burnu wreck off Turkey, with its cargo of at least 306 new Palestinian wine amphorae. As the different examples of contemporary hull construction in Dor demonstrate, various types of craft plied the seas simultaneously. It may be speculated that future shipwreck archaeology will bring to light a stratified hierarchy of ship construction techniques and forms of trade, from the small-scale to the high-level.

The traditional correlation between small ships (evident among the Holy Land evidence: see Table on p. 47) and an increase in private shipping is also somewhat contentious. Although the majority of excavated Byzantine ships are small, medium-sized and large merchant vessels are not unknown. Historical sources refer to 120-ton ships in Belisarius' fleet

4. The shipwrecks of Byzantine Palestine

(Jones 1964: 843), grain ships with a 20,000 measure burden (about 140 tons) were owned by the Church of Alexandria (Monks 1953: 360), and John Moschos described a 35,000 *modii* ship in Palestine (about 250 tons; *Spiritual Meadow* 83; Wortley 1992: 66), the largest recorded Byzantine example. Wrecks off Italy include the 30-m-long seventh-century Pantano Langarini ship, which could have accommodated more than 300 tons of cargo (Throckmorton and Throckmorton 1973: 260, 262) and Le Scole A, dated *c.* AD 365-80, which may have exceeded 33 m in length (Parker 1992a: 391). A 25-m-long vessel probably dating to *c.* AD 320-40 has been excavated at Sobra in Croatia (Parker 1992a: 408).

The small size of most excavated Byzantine ships is hardly surprising, for vessels transporting less than 1,500 amphorae, or 75 tons of cargo, were most common throughout all periods of Antiquity in the Mediterranean (Parker 1992b: 89). Ships with a cargo capacity of 500 tons or more were actually extraordinary and abnormal (Houston 1988: 554-60). The most common class of vessel possessed a burden of 60 tons or less. Prior to constructing models of maritime trade, the question of sample quality requires serious retrospection.

5

Specialised production in the Holy Land

> The ancient economy is an academic battleground. The contestants campaign under various colours – apologists, Marxists, modernizers, primitivists.
>
> Hopkins 1983a: ix

Despite some revealing patterns identified among the Byzantine shipwrecks of Palestine, the undeveloped character of this historical resource is patently obvious. Quite frankly the quality of publications by the IAA, who have surveyed the majority of sites, is generally scandalous. Where data is available, particularly detrimental is the overwhelming trend for interpretation to be site-specific, with no attempt to relate cargo types or domestic assemblage characterisation to provincial agricultural and industrial production structures and to the political economy of the Byzantine state, which is a lively arena of historical debate. Shipwrecks are only one cog in a complex chain of commodity supply, linking farmers, merchants, sea-captains and consumers. Realistically, it is only when cargoes are examined in relation to regional patterns of production that shipwreck economics is explicable, because maritime trade is organically embedded within economies conditioned by socio-political behaviour. As the above quotation from Keith Hopkins' *Trade in the Ancient Economy* demonstrates, in the western Mediterranean this subject is a forum for vibrant discussion, particularly for the Late Roman world, where it is central to one

5. *Specialised production in the Holy Land*

of the great intellectual debates of history: explaining the decline of the Roman Empire.

The interpretation of trade patterns in Byzantine Palestine is complicated by limited research and debate, not only on shipwrecks but also on the economy of the East Mediterranean as a whole in Late Antiquity. Thus, the economic history of the Holy Land is virtually an academic wasteland. Except for generalisations such as the common acceptance that the period was a 'golden age' of agricultural production (Broshi 1984: 29), more penetrating questions addressing economic structures and scales of production are thin on the ground. The few important syntheses (Avi-Yonah 1958; Sperber 1978; Safrai 1994) usually either discuss the subject in relation to Late Roman rabbinical texts, the Theodosian Code and the historical impact of the rise of Christianity, or are simple derivative repetitions of A.H.M. Jones's pioneering research (1964; 1974) which focussed strongly on historical evidence for social caste systems and economic decline caused by high taxation and the over-exploitation of soils.

The theoretical basis behind most studies of the Palestine economy is both methodologically weak and outmoded compared to extant models for the West Mediterranean. Although archaeology has been harnessed to identify specialised forms of regional agricultural and industrial production in the Golan (Urman 1985; Ben David 1998), Samaria (Dar 1986) and around the city of Lod (Schwartz 1991), results are not explained in relation to macro-economic socio-political trends for Palestine or the wider Byzantine Empire.

The dominant model for Byzantine Palestine was conceived by Michael Avi-Yonah who, in a seminal paper (1958), interpreted the economy in relation to the impact of the adoption of Christianity as the official state religion. Avi-Yonah concluded that this remarkable development created an artificial and unsustainable economy. Thus, fourth-century prosperity was stimulated directly by imperial donations, followed by private patronage in the fifth century, with investment directed specifically at ecclesiastical establishments. Following the sack of Rome and the city's depopulation, 'With their jewels handy', envisaged Avi-Yonah (1958: 43), aristocratic western refugees 'could at a moment's notice take ship at Ostia and flee to the East, there to live and build monasteries to their hearts' content'. The capital invested in the construction of ecclesiastical buildings created employment for skilled labourers, whose salaries provided spending power, which in turn stimulated the provincial economy. The export of biblical relics (wood from Christ's cross, saints' bones) and religious gifts for pilgrims constituted a secondary lucrative wave of income (Avi-Yonah 1958: 45-7).

The impact of this 'artificial economy' model has dominated subsequent scholarship on the economy of Byzantine Palestine, with most scholars reiterating Avi-Yonah's argument (Whittaker 1976: 154-5; Gutwein 1981: 266; Garnsey 1998: 158). Thus, Shereshevski (1991: 2) agreed that 'the Byzantine economy suffered from a basic weakness: investment in non-productive buildings such as churches and monasteries provided seasonal work for a great many laborers, but created a dependency on a steady stream of outside capital. Wealth was concentrated in the hands of the non-productive members of society, especially the priesthood. The pendulum of activity swung from trade and finance to the holy sites, Jerusalem in particular.'

Just as primitivists and modernists have tended to paint the ancient economy in black or white tones, so such a theory simplistically – and incorrectly – compartmentalises only one aspect of the Holy Land's economy. Against a strongly political landscape, coupled with the 255 Byzantine churches recorded in Israel (Ovadiah 1993), the traditional preoccupation with religion in archaeology is historically understandable. How-

5. Specialised production in the Holy Land

ever, modern approaches clearly demonstrate that investment in land and agriculture comprised the single most important source of investment and income in antiquity. Correspondingly, archaeological evidence for such development is the crucial gauge of scales and structures of economic complexity. If the limitations of shipwreck archaeology have so far failed to illuminate the economic rationale underlying inter-regional trade, what can land-based archaeology contribute to the debate? Despite the absence of trade models in the East Mediterranean in general, the huge quantity of excavation and survey work conducted in Israel nevertheless enables relevant sources to be synthesised.

Numerous inter-related questions require addressing before the overall character of the role of maritime trade within the economy of Byzantine Palestine can be understood, even in simplistic terms. Key questions include:

(i) What range of products was manufactured in Palestine for export markets?
(ii) What were the social or religious contexts of production?
(iii) To what degree did city life dominate the rural sector?
(iv) Were cities parasitic consumers of rural production?
(v) What was the character of rural production: subsistence farming, surplus production?
(vi) To what degree was the Holy Land's economy inter-dependent or dependent on imports?
(vii) What scales of manufacture co-existed?
(viii) How did the rhythms of production change between *c.* AD 320 and 640 and when did classical forms of trade cease?
(ix) What were the scales of inter-regional trade and what was the geographical distribution of produce?
(x) What forms of exchange prevailed in Byzantine Palestine (open trade or state-dominated exchange)?

Addressing all these questions is a monumental task well beyond the parameters of this book. The following debate examines aspects of these taxing issues by focusing on three different forms of economic activity in Byzantine Palestine: glass processing, cloth and dye manufacture, and wine production. The latter is especially important for providing archaeological evidence for scales and structures of production and export.

Specialised agricultural and industrial production

Ancient Palestine, as the Bible metaphorically confirms, was immensely fertile, flowing with milk and honey. In the Byzantine period this highly geographically diverse land was exploited to a level unsurpassed until the twentieth century. Soils supported the cultivation of abundant cereals, vegetables, fruits and spices, and Talmudic literature refers to some 500 types of Palestinian agricultural produce (Broshi 1986; Safrai 1994; Dar 1995; Dauphin 1998). As in all other Mediterranean regions, wheat, olives and grapes were the three most commonly grown and consumed crops, essential to the daily diet. Polyculture was considered the economic ideal and most farmers pursued mixed cultivation. Thus, in the first two decades of the third century, Rabbi Yohanan wrote that 'Blessed art thou in the field – that your properties should be divided into three parts: one third grain, one third olives, and one third grapes' (*B. Bava Mezi'a* 107a, Deuteronomy 28:3; Sperber 1978: 191). A Christian inscription bordered by crosses within a late fifth-century villa at Caesarea follows a similar formula: 'The Lord God will bless your grain and your wine and your oil and He will increase [them]' (Siegelmann 1974: 218). Excavations conducted in the Jewish village of Sumaqa (Dar 1999), Samaritan Antesion (Ayalon *et al.* 1994) and Christian Khirbet Zikhrin (Fischer 1994) indicate that the joint cultivation of these three

5. Specialised production in the Holy Land

staple crops was practised by farmers irrespective of religious background.

The area under cultivation in Palestine expanded considerably in Late Antiquity. Although a terraced landscape first developed as predetermined units in the Iron Age II period (eighth to sixth centuries BC), peak terracing development occurred in the Byzantine period, when an estimated 50% of the central highlands was terraced and cultivated (Gibson 1995: 173-7). Pottery scatters deposited with domestic refuse in fields to manure soils were quantified during the archaeological survey of the Dor landscape and suggested that 29% of the pottery from all fields dated to the Early Roman period and that 48% was Byzantine (Gibson and Kingsley, unpublished data). Increased cultivation in Late Antiquity is consistent with population increase (see Chapter 1).

In some regions cultivation benefited from improved engineering techniques. Former swamplands around the city of Apollonia were freed for cultivation following the reclamation of land by quarrying a 190-m-long tunnel through the rocky foothills (Tsuk and Ayalon 1995: 140-1), enabling the brackish waters stagnating in troughs between sandstone ridges to seep into the sea. Extensive tracts of the Negev Desert were made fertile as flash-flood farming was perfected along *wadi* beds. Large sets of stone masonry dams, such as seven extending along 22 km of the Nahal Hevron (Negev 1997: 128, 131), were constructed to regulate the flow of water into agricultural fields and to prevent soil erosion.

Alongside the 'holy trinity' of wine, oil and wheat, specialised forms of large-scale industrial production in Byzantine Palestine included cloth manufacture and dye processing, glass production and the blowing of vessels, pottery manufacture, and fish farming. All of these activities seem to occur at far greater scales and with far greater complexity than in preceding periods. But what evidence can be harnessed to assess scales of production?

Glass production

Fourteen sites specialising in glass production have been published from Byzantine Palestine. The manufacture of glass vessels was common in *Palaestina Prima* and *Secunda*, between the Galilee and central coastal area, and was not restricted to sites of a particular religious or urban status. The production of glass involved two basic stages. First, raw glass was cast in large blocks, which were broken into small, transportable amorphous ingots. Secondly, glass cullet was remelted and blown into vessels. The structure of the Palestinian glass industry demonstrates how some settlements of different status were economically inter-linked: some villages only produced raw glass, which seems to have been sold commercially in cities. Other rural estates and towns both processed cullet and manufactured glass vessels.

Raw glass was produced in various types of settlement, ranging in status from the village to the city. Waste from a possible fourth- or fifth-century glass kiln has been identified in the Jewish village of Sumaqa in the Carmel (Dar 1999) and glass slag has been recorded in the small town of coastal Sucumina (Hirschfeld 1998: 20). Industrial glass waste from Horvat Qav is associated with a farmhouse of the seventh and eighth centuries (Gorin-Rosen and Stern 1995: 17-18). Although some of this material may have been exported, scales of production are unclear and this industry probably served only local demands.

A far larger enterprise was a workshop in an estate at Jalame in the lower Galilee producing bowls, jugs, bottles, lamps, jars and *amphoriskoi* (Weinberg and Goldstein 1988: 38). The circular furnace measured about 2.4 x 3.6 m and is

5. Specialised production in the Holy Land

dated by coins to between AD 351 and 383 (although these issues will have remained in circulation throughout the fifth century). The workshop's dump extended over 150 m² (Weinberg 1988: 28) and production was clearly geared to intra-regional trade. Another Byzantine rural estate has been excavated at Horvat Rakit in the Carmel and also incorporated both stages of glass vessel production, although apparently only for localised use by Samaritan communities for purposes of maintaining ritual purity (personal communication, S. Dar, August 1997).

The manufacture of both cullet and vessels was also practised in larger settlements. The Jewish town of Beth She'arim in the Galilee was renowned for its glassworks from the fourth century onward (Vitto 1996: 140-1) and the massive scale of production is exemplified by a nine-ton glass slab recorded inside a melting-tank (Brill 1965). A slab of comparable size has been excavated in the city of Apollonia within a 2.50 x 3.80 m melting chamber (Gorin-Rosen 2002: 9). The demand for wood to fuel furnaces for the glass industry in this city has been interpreted as causing the disappearance of the region's wooded landscape: oak accounted for 66% of sampled species in the Greek period, but only 5% of samples in Byzantine levels (Gophna and Ayalon 1989: 25). Glass furnaces have also been recorded at Akko (Schwartz 1998: 171).

Evidence of specialisation in glass vessel manufacture only is known from several other urban settlements. A workshop producing polycandelon lamps, wine goblets, spherical bottles, juglets, bowls and window glass has been excavated adjacent to a sixth-century 'bazaar' along the north-east city wall at Scythopolis (Mazor and Bar-Nathan 1998: 28). The stems of about 400 bowl-shaped glass lamps excavated in the shadow of the Byzantine city wall at Caesarea (Peleg and Reich 1992: 155, 158) almost certainly originated from a nearby, unexcavated glass workshop. Whether these cities purchased raw glass, or whether cullet was processed in unexcavated city districts, is currently unclear. Based on the above evidence, either scenario is theoretically possible.

An unusual context of cullet manufacture has been recorded at coastal Bet Eli'ezer, about 8 km south of Caesarea, which represents the largest known example of production in Israel. Seventeen single-use Late Byzantine glass kilns consisted of twin firing furnaces and a rectangular melting chamber (2.00 x 4.00 m), each capable of producing a maximum of between eight and ten tons of glass in a single firing (Gorin-Rosen 1995: 42-3). The absence of distorted glass wasters at the site, and indeed any traces of settlement, seem to indicate that only ingots were produced at this artisanal centre. Similar manufacture centres have been surveyed along the Sharon Plain, all sharing the attributes of highly specialised operations producing highest quality shades of transparent green and blue glass containing few bubbles or impurities (Gorin-Rosen 2002: 12).

Unlike dyed cloth, glass manufacture is not referred to in Late Antique historical texts and state legislation, such as the *Expositio Totius Mundi et Gentium* or the Theodosian Code, and it may be assumed that production and sale was mainly, if not completely, commercial. Glass slag recorded in a late sixth- to early seventh-century commercial district in the city of Sepphoris in the Galilee (Meyers *et al.* 1995: 70) and in Late Byzantine shops just outside the city wall of Jerusalem (Maeir 1994: 302) constitutes evidence for the retail sale of glass ingots. Although the scale of production in Palestine was substantial, its importance within the overall economy is not easily assessed. Vessels blown in workshops at Scythopolis consisted of the most common types used in daily life (Mazor and Bar-Nathan 1998: 29) and would have predominantly served the local communities. Although no Palestinian glass vessels have been recorded on Byzantine shipwrecks, the presence of ingots

5. Specialised production in the Holy Land

in the anchorages of the Holy Land does hint at some long-distance commercial export.

Cloth manufacture and dye processing

Cloth and linen weaving and dyeing were traditional Palestinian industrial activities practised along the coastal plain since the thirteenth century BC (Karmon 1992: 58; Karmon and Spanier 1988: 186). Various forms of cloth manufacture, dye production and tanning existed in Byzantine Palestine in both rural and urban contexts.

Murex shells and bone needles, possibly used to extract snails from shells, have been excavated in the Christian town of Capernaum and may originate from a small purple-dye production workshop (Tzaferis and Peleg 1990: 109). The inland location of this Galilean site, about 48 km east of the Mediterranean Sea where the murex originates, is an interesting indication of the potential profit to be derived from this industry. Archaeological evidence for the processing of flax or dyes has been recorded at seven non-urban sites in Israel. Some are clearly located in a rural environment, although reports fail to describe whether the context is a village, estate or farm. An inscription on a *tabula ansata* from Khirbet Dah-Dah in the countryside of North Hebron dated to AD 527 refers to the 'shed of Zenonos the tanner from Ascalon'. Rock-cut installations scattered over 460 m^2 around the inscription, including six rectangular basins, were probably used to steep skins and perhaps dye cloth (Amit 1991: 162).

Alongside these rural sites, cities dominated large-scale cloth and dye production. The most substantial dye workshop recorded in Israel is a mid-fifth century site excavated at Constantia (modern Gaza). Eight plastered pools and basins for crushing dyes extend over 250-300 m^2 adjacent to a synagogue, which may provide an indication that production was controlled by Jewish artisans and merchants. Chemical analysis of reddish-brown and violet pigments from this installation traced the raw materials used to manufacture the dyes to the Negev, Sinai, Italy and Greece (Ovadiah 1969: 196-7). The Gaza dyeworks were evidently a large capital investment whose owners had intimate contacts with merchants in the western Mediterranean. Dyed clothing must have been exported from here as a high value primary cargo, probably on merchant vessels trading local wine packaged in LR4 Palestinian amphorae.

Talmudic literature refers to purple dye production in Diospolis (Schwartz 1991: 173). This city, as well as those of Caesarea and Neapolis, are also listed as exporters of cloth died purple in the *Expositio Totius Mundi et Gentium*, issued in AD 359 (*Expositio* XXXI; Rougé 1966: 165). An industrial complex at Dor consisting of a central structure, open courtyard and water conduit leading to three rock-cut basins has also been identified as a purple-dye factory operating in the fourth and sixth centuries (Raban 1995: 301). Scythopolis was the most famous Palestinian city involved in cloth manufacture, and the *Expositio Totius Mundi et Gentium* refers to abundant cloth production in this city and its export throughout the world (*Expositio* XXXI; Rougé 1966: 165). Heavily plastered brick-built basins containing draining vents and inter-connected by ceramic pipes overlying the threshold of the dismantled triple gateway in the *propylaeum* area of the city, dating to the second half of the fourth century (Foerster and Tsafrir 1993: 12; Tsafrir and Foerster 1994: 103), are probably related to this industry.

Although no inscriptions describing the administration or organisation of dye and cloth production in Byzantine Palestine have been discovered, historical texts suggest that at least some urban operations were state-controlled. Thus, a law in the Theodosian Code, issued in AD 385, ordains that 'if any person should dare to usurp the use of a boat that is assigned to the compulsory public service of purple dye collection and to the

5. Specialised production in the Holy Land

collection of shellfish, he shall be held liable to the payment of two pounds of gold' (*CTh*. 10.20.12; Pharr 1952: 287). But by the first half of the fifth century the state's attempt to monopolise the purple-dye industry appears to have become less effective. Another edict in the Theodosian Code, dated to AD 436, refers to 300 lbs of purple silk that had been 'coloured in clandestine dyeing operations'. The state was so disturbed by this illegal activity that it implemented the extraordinary measure of sending every seventh man from the bureau of secretaries, every sixth man from the bureau of regular taxes and every fifth man from the bureau of registrars to investigate dyeworks in Phoenicia (*CTh*. 10.20.18; Pharr 1952: 288). Whether centralised control over purple-dye production was secured after this date is uncertain, but this pattern dovetails interestingly with increased evidence from shipwrecks for medium-level merchants in shipping.

The Theodosian Code also suggests that linen production was state-controlled in parts of Palestine, at least in the Early Byzantine period. An edict issued in AD 374 fined anyone illegally sheltering linen workers at Scythopolis 5 lbs of gold (*CTh*. 10.20.8; Pharr 1952: 286). This law is interpreted as a reaction to state workers attempting to escape Late Antiquity's enforced hereditary caste system (Avi-Yonah 1962: 134).

Several Palestinian cities clearly manufactured large quantities of dye and cloth, but the actual scale of production remains a matter of conjecture. If papyrological evidence from Egypt is applicable to the Holy Land, then urban cloth manufacture was already big business in the Roman period. At Oxyrhynchos as many as 2,000 garments were exported during a five-day period in the third century, which suggests a possible annual production figure of about 80,000 garments (Bagnall 1993: 82-3). Historical texts confirm that at least some cloth produced and dyed in Byzantine Palestine was exported. No evidence for this activity has been recorded on the Byzantine

Shipwreck Archaeology

shipwrecks of Israel, which highlights the limitations of relying on this source and the necessity to be aware of archaeologically invisible products. Instead, we must rely on a fusion of archaeological and historical evidence to reconstruct the character, structure and scale of this industry.

Palestinian wine production and export

Wine's basic nutritional value provided an estimated quarter of the daily caloric intake and about a third of the body's iron requirements in the Roman and Byzantine periods (Broshi 1986: 46) and thus generated a massive demand. At least 60 types of different wines co-existed with different maturities and tastes, some simple, others more exotic, mixed with balsam, honey, pepper, myrrh and wood (*Bab. T., Gittin* 70a; Broshi 1984: 26; Frankel 1999: 198-204). Current estimates suggest that men consumed between 146 and 182 litres of undiluted wine every year and that intake levels among women comprised half that amount (Tchernia 1986: 26). Assuming a population of a million people, Palestine may have consumed a staggering 73 million litres of undiluted wine annually in Late Antiquity (about 3.2 million amphorae of 23 litre average capacity).

The huge number of rock-cut wine presses preserved in Israel enables the structure and scale of this specific form of specialised production to be analysed in remarkable detail. The total quantity of ancient wine presses extant probably numbers tens of thousands (Frankel 1999: 51), with some 899 currently datable to the Byzantine period (Kingsley 2001: 49; Fig. 17). (The vast majority remain undated.) As would be expected in a highly sophisticated industry, pressing installations display notable diversity in shape, size and technology. Examples invariably incorporated at least one treading-floor sloping down to a collecting vat, both plastered and tessellated, with a decan-

5. Specialised production in the Holy Land

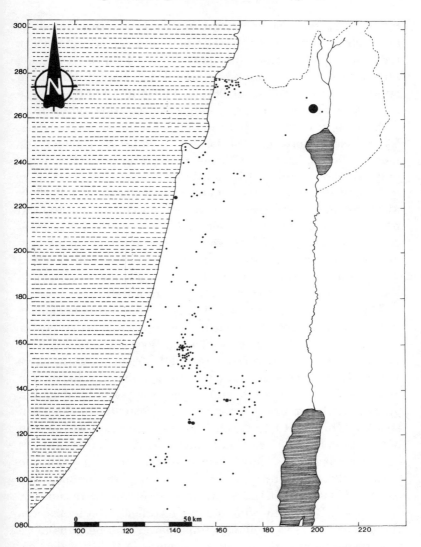

Fig. 17. Distribution map of Byzantine wine presses in Israel (excluding the Negev).

tation sump between these features to receive residual skins and stalks. More complex presses might incorporate side niches for fermenting grapes before pressing, lead pipes to channel juice into vats, and painted or moulded plaster. Distribution studies suggest that about 95% of Palestine's wine seems to have been produced along a long rural belt extending from Nahariyya in northern Palestine to Ashkelon and Jerusalem. Large installations are also located in *Palaestina Tertia*, the modern Negev, near the cities of Elusa (Mazar 1981: 51), Sobata (Mayerson 1985: 76-7) and Eboda (Tahal 1995: 131).

Most pressing was undertaken by simple treading underfoot. More complex installations were equipped with mechanical pressing apparatus. The 'lever and press' method was most common and employed a wooden infrastructure overlying baskets of grapes, which were squeezed under the pressure exerted by a beam pulled down manually (or using stone weights) and wedged at one end into a niche in the press wall.

The most complex type of Byzantine wine press is characterised by a screw system identifiable by a mortise cut or inserted into the middle of a treading-floor (Figs 18-20). This apparatus was used to squeeze residual juice out of grape skins and stalks after treading. The technology, layout, construction quality and efficiency of this press type is superior to 'lever and press' installations. Screw installations excavated at the farmstead at Khirbet Hilal near Jerusalem, associated with a coin of Constans I, AD 337-41 (Amit 1992: 150-1), and another from the estate at Jalame, dated numismatically to *c.* AD 350 at the earliest (Weinberg 1988: 11-15; Fig. 19), suggest that operation became widespread in the second quarter of the fourth century. Some 9% of Byzantine wine presses recorded in Israel possess this technology. Less reliant on manpower and perhaps more prestigious to own, the screw press seems to reflect intensive, efficient large-scale wine production. However, these installa-

5. Specialised production in the Holy Land

Fig. 18. A Byzantine wine press from Tel Qasile, with a reconstructed wooden screw apparatus in the treading-floor. Grapes were left to sweeten in the side niches.

tions are encountered in most types of settlements, including villages, estates and monasteries.

The average wine press comprised a treading-floor measuring 3.4 x 3.6 m and a collecting-vat 1.3 x 1.7 m and 1.1 m deep. If the vat of an average-sized installation was full, a single pressing could have produced just over 2,400 litres of wine (105 amphorae). About 42% of presses are large-scale installations exceeding this average size and their vats were capable of holding between 4,000 and 59,000 litres (174 and 2,565 amphorae). Again, these large-scale presses are not restricted to sites of a specific status, but occur in a variety of contexts (Kingsley 2001: 49).

Large-scale wine presses include an example associated with a fourth-century farmstead at Khirbet Hilal in the Jerusalem zone, capable of processing over 9,000 litres in one pressing (Amit 1992: 150-1). A vat in the monastery of Caparbaricha in

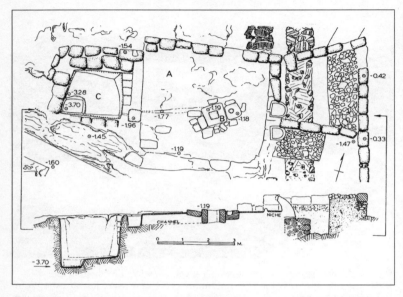

Fig. 19. Plan of a fourth-century wine press with screw system from Jalame: treading-floor (A), screw-mortise (B) and collecting-vat (C) (after Weinberg 1988: fig. 2.4).

the Jerusalem region held more than 6,800 litres (Hirschfeld 1992: 108), and three large wine presses associated with the monastery of Pisgat Ze'ev could each process between 8,500 and 9,100 litres of wine (Seligman 1994: 52-4; Shourkin 1997: 99). The largest Byzantine wine press known from Israel is the fourth-century installation located at coastal Achziv in the Nahariyya region, which possessed three treading floors and two vats, with a combined production capacity of 59,000 litres (Syon 1998: 7).

The remote Jewish village of Sumaqa (Dar 1999), located among steep-sided mountains and deep ravines in the Carmel, is a fascinating site that challenges our preconceptions about contexts of specialised wine production Three fourth- and fifth-century installations have a combined capacity of 46,463 litres

5. Specialised production in the Holy Land

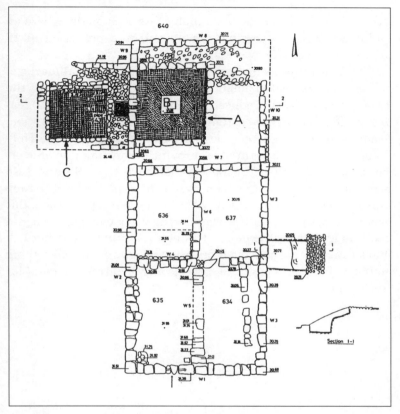

Fig. 20. Fourth- or fifth-century wine press with screw system from the Jewish village of Sumaqa: tessellated treading-floor (A), screw-mortise (B) and tessellated collecting-vat (C). Associated with a structure, possibly a storeroom (after Dar 1999).

(the equivalent of about 2,323 local amphorae; Fig. 20). If the vats were filled only twice during consecutive phases of seasonal use, surplus wine would have been obtained. If the installations were used three times during the harvest season, 64% of the wine produced would have been surplus (Kingsley 1999a: 74). Interestingly, wine production was a secondary economic pursuit for the 900 inhabitants of Sumaqa, where an unknown product (possibly almond oil) was processed in 12 major, yet enigmatic, workshops.

The Palestinian wine industry contains all the hallmarks of a highly sophisticated business very clearly geared towards the creation of surplus produce. But in isolation its domestic features offer no obvious insights into contexts of consumption, leaving unanswered the question of to what extent the Holy Land's vines were nurtured for provincial consumption or overseas markets. When considered alongside the LR4 and LR5 wine amphorae so common on Byzantine shipwrecks off Israel, the balance is tipped in favour of at least some export trade. But what quantity of produce was destined for overseas? Such a focus is in fact best explored through the humble potsherd. If Palestinian wines travelled far and wide, amphora packaging found on land sites ought to serve as a crucial trace element for such trade.

6

Exports, imports and the balance of trade

Elements of glass, cloth, dye and wine production all display different weighted indications of mass processing, but in isolation cannot tell us why and for whom such specialist production developed. The assumption that the combined attributes of large-scale manufacture and the coastal locations of many glass and dye workshops must have been geared toward some international trade hardly requires a bold leap of faith, but is far too tenuous to serve as the main structure for an economic model.

So how do we define the complexity of such obvious mass production with greater precision? While one node of assessment is the context of manufacture, the other is demand: geographical penetration, volumes of diffusion, and the chronology of produce export. No research has so far sampled the chemical composition of glass vessels outside Palestine for provenance studies and, bearing in mind the tendency for glass ingots from different sources to be inter-mixed, often with remelted vessels, the short-term potential of such a line of enquiry is not promising. Since cloth is not preserved within most Mediterranean climates, this source also has to be excluded. Instead, we are compelled to turn to the land-based study of pottery distributions and quantification, the optimum methodology available for examining Palestinian exports. Produced and discarded in massive volumes, pottery's virtually indestructible preservation in the archaeological record facilitates relative standardised and objective analyses.

Export markets

Markets located throughout the Mediterranean basin and further afield were highly receptive to Palestinian wine amphorae (Figs 21-2). To the south LR4 containers poured through the port of Alexandria, accounting for 73% of all amphorae in some sixth- to seventh-century contexts (Majcherek 1992: 106, 116-17). Beyond this coastal gateway hundreds of LR4 were stocked in the royal tombs of Ballana in lower Egypt (Kirwin 1938: pl. 111, no. 10) and were transported even further south to Masira Island off the coast of south Oman (Whitcomb forthcoming: n. 31) and into the Yemenite port of Qana (Sedov 1992: fig. 2, nos 1 and 5).

Between this extreme and the northern periphery of distribution at Wroxeter in Britain (Riley 1979: 220-2) Palestinian amphorae crop up in almost all excavated Mediterranean sites of Late Antique date and in varied contexts. Urban consumption is represented by discarded amphorae recorded throughout Carthage (Peacock 1984: table 1; Tomber 1988b: 497; Freed 1993a: 85; Opait 1998: pl. 1, no. 17), at Pella in Jordan (McNicoll *et al.* 1992: pl. 115, no. 5), in Turkey within a bathhouse at Pergamon (Atik 1995: 195) and within the early seventh-century shops at Sardis (Stephens Crawford 1990: 97). In Greece they turn up within the great cities of Athens and Corinth (Johnson 1986: 591-3). Further west, Palestinian imports are highly conspicuous in the Italian cities of Naples (Arthur 1985: 250-5), Ravenna (Maioli and Stoppioni 1989: 573), Ostia (Martin 1998: 389) and throughout Rome (Carignani and Pacetti 1989: 8-11). An equally broad distribution exists in the French cities of Arles (Congès and Leguilloux 1991: 218), Lyon, Narbonne (Bonifay and Villedieu 1989: 18) and

6. Exports, imports and the balance of trade

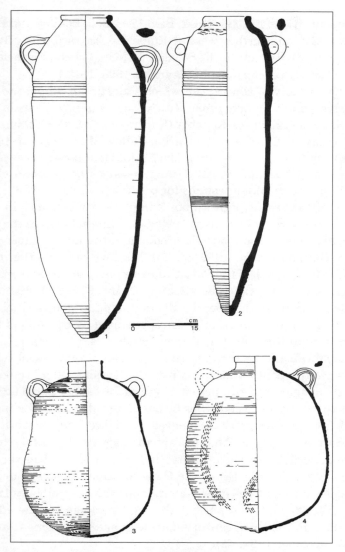

Fig. 21. Palestinian LR4 (nos 1-2) and LR5 bag-shaped amphorae (nos 3-4) (after Dothan and Freedman 1967: 69; Tubb 1986: 52; Johnson 1988: fig. 7.53, no. 807; Gichon 1993: taf. 20, no. 3).

Marseille (Bonifay 1986: 291-2; Bien 1998: 282; Bonifay and Piéri 1995: 112) and further west at Emporiae, Tarraco (Keay 1984: 76-7, 357-8), Benalua, Calle Soledad, El Monastil and Plaza de los Tres Reyes in eastern Spain (Reynolds 1995: 181-2).

The variety of contexts in which Palestinian amphorae are excavated is similarly broad. In Cyprus examples occur in the basilica of Kalavasos-Kopetra (Rautman *et al.* 1993: 234) and the village of Petrera in the Maroni Valley (Manning *et al.* 1994: 366), while examples excavated at Agios Georgios to the west of the island had apparently been re-used as bee-hives and as feeding and drinking troughs for poultry (Bakirtzis 1996: 158). In Constantinople Palestinian wines were consumed in the church of Saraçhane (Hayes 1992: 65), while soldiers in the fort of Chios enjoyed comparable products in the mid-seventh century (Ballance *et al.* 1989: pl. 25). Military consumption may also explain much of the Palestinian amphora shipments reaching Histria near the Black Sea (Scorpan 1977: 273, 293) and nine locations in the Danube Basin in Upper Moesia (Bjelajac 1996: 49). Elite consumption is represented by the villa of San Giovanni di Ruoti in Italy (Freed 1994b: 394, no. 158).

Quantification – the objective assessment of a vessel type's relative frequency amongst a pottery deposit – offers the optimum insight into the actual rhythms of export between the fourth and seventh centuries by enabling volumes deposited in different centuries to be compared. Evidence from the both the eastern and western Mediterranean suggests that LR4 export commenced at an earlier date than the trade in bag-shaped amphorae. Thus in Egypt the Gaza/Ashkelon type was deposited in a burial at Tell el-Maskhuta *c*. AD 125-60 (Holladay 1982: 43, fig. 62) and was part of the food package consumed by workers in the third-century marble quarries at Mons Claudianus (Tomber 1996: 45).

The level of Palestinian wine amphorae exported before *c*. AD 400 seems to have been limited. At Porto Torres in Sardinia

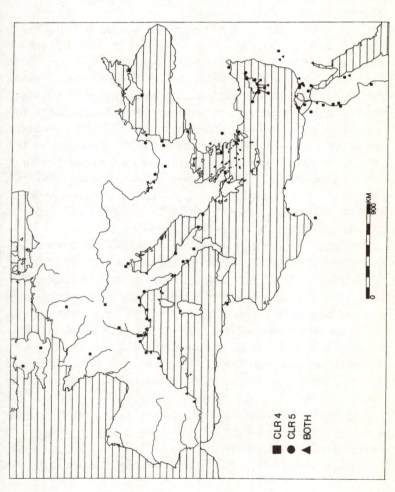

Fig. 22. Distribution map of Palestinian amphorae exported from the Holy Land (fourth to seventh centuries AD).

they represent only 1.3% of all amphorae between *c.* 350 and 400 (Reynolds 1995: 313-15; Villedieu 1984: 175-6), and 3% between AD 390 and 420 in the Temple of Magna Mater in Rome (Carignani and Pacetti 1989: 11). Palestinian wine amphorae account for a paltry 0.21% of the 6,796 sherds excavated in the late fourth- to early fifth-century deposits in Carthage's Circus (Tomber 1988b: 497).

Large-scale export took off between *c.* AD 400 and 450. Insufficient numbers of deposits of overlapping date have been excavated in the Mediterranean to assess subtle fluctuations in the scale of long-distance trade during the Byzantine period, but quantified data currently point to regular and continuous wine export until the mid-seventh century. By the early fifth century Palestinian imports accounted for 12.1% of all amphorae at Arles (Congès and Leguilloux 1991). By the mid-fifth century 44.7% of containers in different sectors of Carthage derived from the Holy Land (Hayes 1980: 205; Riley 1981: 90). Even some 9% of amphorae shipped into Tarragona between 450 and 475 (Reynolds 1995: 180, 282-3) and 8.5% in Naples *c.* 500 (Arthur 1985: 252) were from Palestine.

Between the fifth and sixth centuries Holy Land wines imported into Argos rose from 15% to 20% (Abadie 1989: 54), and no abatement is visible until the mid-seventh century. Certainly, Palestinian production comprised 15.3% of amphorae in parts of Carthage between the late sixth and early seventh centuries (Riley 1981: 103), 13% at Calle Soledad in Spain between 575 and 621 (Reynolds 1995: 182, 264-5), 19.8% in Marseille between the late sixth and early seventh centuries (Bonifay 1986: 303-4), and 11% at the Schola Praeconum in Rome *c.* 600-50 (Whitehouse *et al.* 1985: 186).

Although current trends in scholarship favour the hypothesis of a prolonged survival of classical forms of Romanised administration and culture into the Early Islamic period in the Near East (Kennedy 1985; Whitcomb 1995), substantial ce-

6. Exports, imports and the balance of trade

ramic evidence opposes this model. Late contexts do include deposits dated from 650 to *c.* 700 at Carthage (Hayes 1978: fig. 13, nos 48-9), 655-70 in Constantinople (Hayes 1992: 100, fig. 47, no. 166 and fig. 48, no. 172), *c.* 642-60 in the fortress at Chios (Boardman 1989: pl. 25), and dated 666 in the basilica at Ayios Philon in Cyprus (du Plat Taylor and Megaw 1981: 219, fig. 42, no. 361). No certain examples of exported Palestinian amphorae date later than AD 670. Certainly the latest quantified deposit recorded, at Ostrakine in northern Sinai, demonstrates that LR4 imports had declined from 63% between *c.* 550 and the early seventh century to 15% of all amphorae *c.* 650-85 (Oked 1996: 168-9).

Equally significant is the transformation in production methods (shape, fabric and vessel size) experienced in Early Islamic Palestinian bag-shaped LR5 amphorae. Whereas Byzantine merchants had optimised amphorae to suit sea trade (short rims were less susceptible to breakage and body ribbing was designed to facilitate rope bindings; Fig. 21, no. 4) this trend was reversed in the Umayyad period, indicating a radical shift away from traditional orders of commerce. In particular, rims double in height and body ribbing disappeared: the sign of functional change away from seaborne trade.

Key pottery assemblages quantified from several provinces, most notably Tunisia, Italy and France, have demonstrated that the frequency of Palestinian amphorae recorded overseas varies considerably, even within an individual city or archaeological site. But on average between *c.* AD 450 and 650 Palestinian amphorae accounted for 10.7% of all Byzantine amphorae recovered in individual sites at Carthage, 8.2% in Rome, and 6.8% in Marseille (Kingsley 1999a: 175). Superficially these figures may seem small, but what volume of wine export and consumption might they represent?

Calculating orders of magnitude is complicated by many variables capable of distorting results. Some pottery assemblages sampled may be the accumulated refuse of decades, even a century, and in some circumstances residuality may prevent comprehension of how quantities of different amphora types changed through time at a site. Understanding the selection process that culminated in the deposition and mixing of domestic refuse is also largely unknown. However, the random processes affecting assemblage composition are likely to have been equal for all types of amphorae in homogeneous deposits, and statistics procured by pottery quantification may therefore be considered an important guide to consumption rates. Although the criticism that pottery quantification only indicates long-term trends is not entirely invalid, this methodology is the only analytic and standardised tool available to historians and archaeologists alike that progresses the debate beyond the highly impressionistic. Scholars of ancient trade have welcomed this tool with open arms.

Converting percentages of Palestinian amphorae into wine consumption figures requires access to ancient urban population figures, which are notoriously difficult to estimate. Estimates of the population of Carthage suggest that the city declined from a third of a million people during the first century (Raven 1984: 124) to about 100,000 in the fourth century (Lepelley 1981: 48). As we have seen, using historical references and early modern comparative data, Tchernia (1986: 26) has estimated that men consumed between 146 litres and 182 litres of undiluted wine annually during the Roman period, and that women generally drank less than half the male equivalent. Information describing the ratio of men to women and children in Roman and Byzantine society is rarely discussed in studies of ancient demography (cf. Eyben 1980-1; Frier 1982), but as an approximate guide this model will assume that men, women and children each constituted a third of the population in Late Antiquity. The resultant statistics are likely to constitute mini-

6. Exports, imports and the balance of trade

mal figures, rather than the maximum, because Tchernia's lower figure of 146 litres is used.

Based on a minimum annual estimate of 146 litres of wine consumption, it may be proposed that 33,333 men consumed 4.87 million litres of wine per annum at Carthage. If the female population used half this quantity, a total adult annual consumption of 7.3 million litres can be assumed. Using 10.7% as an average figure of Palestinian amphora import in Byzantine Carthage, it is possible to argue that this city habitually imported 781,092 litres of Palestinian wine annually between c. 450 and the early seventh century. The combined average capacity of an LR4 and LR5 amphora is about 23 litres (Zemer 1977: 66-9), equating to an annual import of 33,960 amphorae. This is the equivalent of 31 annual shipments in a 20 m long merchant vessel containing a cargo of 1,100 amphorae, all of Palestinian origin.

A similar model can be formulated for Rome. Durliat's study of the capital's population (1990: 112, 117) proposes a composition of 350,000 people between the early and mid-fifth century, which declined to 60,000 by about AD 530. Excluding the deposit dated to between c. 600-50 at the Schola Praeconum, where Palestinian products account for 11% of all amphorae (Whitehouse et al. 1985), Palestinian amphorae from five other quantified assemblages which fall within this earlier time-span represent an average of 5.9%. The model proposed here therefore suggests that Rome may have received 1.5 million litres of Palestinian wine every year (65,500 amphorae) between the early and mid-fifth century, and 481,800 litres (21,000 amphorae) during the first half of the seventh century. These figures are the equivalent of 59 fifth-century shipments and 19 shipments during the seventh century. Although it is conceivable that some maritime cargoes transported to Rome may only have contained Palestinian amphorae, no wreck containing such a primary cargo has been recorded in the western Mediterranean. More likely would have been the transport west of Palestinian wine as secondary consignments among a composite cargo, as was the case on a sixth-century ship wrecked at La Palud off southern France (Long and Volpe 1998: 337-8). (The above figures are rounded up and down.)

Import markets: amphorae

A model arguing for a long-lived, extensive Palestinian export market as a fundamental aspect of the Holy Land's economy is a far cry from the image of a province dependent on the flow of ecclesiastical patronage, which remains common currency within the archaeology of Byzantine Palestine. But how can we determine whether sea-trade generated broad-based generalised prosperity in the Holy Land, rather than merely enabling the social elite to expand their wealth and investment portfolios? Once again, pottery in the form of imported amphorae and fine-wares provides the only objective answer.

Imported amphorae have been recorded on 87 sites throughout Israel between Shelomi to the north of the country, as far east as Hammat Gader on the south-east shore of the Sea of Galilee, and as south as the fortress at 'Ein Hazeva in the Arava Valley, located 112 km inland. Fifteen types of amphora produced in the eastern Mediterranean (between Egypt and Greece) and 23 types imported from the western Mediterranean (North Africa, Spain/Portugal) have been identified (Kingsley 1999a: 165; Figs 23-8).

An immediate and revealing pattern is that imports occur on sites of different religious and social status from the urban to the rural and on Christian, Jewish and Samaritan settlements. No clustering on high-status settlements is apparent. Non-local amphorae occur in 22 urban contexts, six towns, and 12 rural sites (four villages, two agricultural estates, one watch-booth, two farms, and three undefined sites). The detailed focus of

6. Exports, imports and the balance of trade

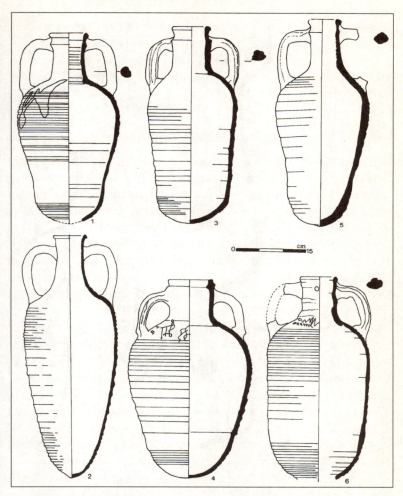

Fig. 23. Byzantine LR1 imported amphorae found in Israel: Caesarea, Scythopolis, Tel Masos, Jerusalem, Caesarea and Ashdod (after Raban *et al.* 1993: 97, no. 1; Fitzgerald 1931: pl. 31, no. 27; Fritz and Kempinski 1983: 213, no. 10; Crowfoot and Fitzgerald 1927: pl. 14, no. 29; Adan-Bayewitz 1986: 124, no. 4; Dothan and Freedman 1967: 69, no. 2.)

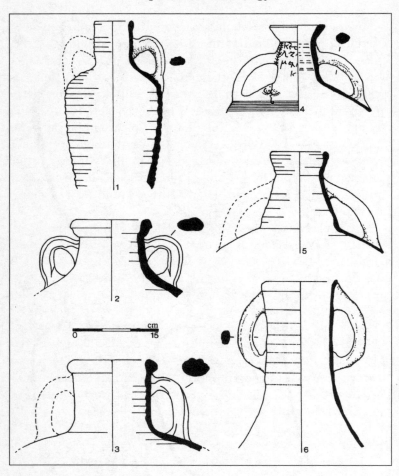

Fig. 24. Imported Byzantine amphorae found in Israel: LR7 (no. 1, Caesarea); Keay III (no. 2, Apollonia), Keay IV (no. 3, Apollonia), LR2 (nos 4-5, Upper Zohar and Jerusalem), Egyptian Type A (no. 6, Dor). (After Adan-Bayewitz 1986: 124, no. 13; Roll and Ayalon 1989: fig. 87, no. 4; 1989: fig. 76, no. 6; Harper 1995: 132, no. 145; Magness 1992: 152, no. 3; Kingsley and Raveh 1996: fig. 35, P22.)

6. Exports, imports and the balance of trade

fieldwork on Jewish settlements (compared to Samaritan sites) provides a clear indication of an engagement in long-distance trade. Imports occur in the Jewish villages of Khirbet Shema, Gush Halav and Meiron, the synagogue of Kyrios Leontis at Scythopolis, and in a Jewish catacomb at Bet Shearim of the first half of the fourth century (Kingsley 1999a: 165). A wide variety of LR1, LR2, LR3, Keay XXVG, Beirut amphorae and a Coptic vessel were excavated at the Jewish village of Sumaqa (Kingsley 1999b). These imports are particularly important for conclusively laying to rest the argument that all Jewish communities shied away from long-distance trade for reasons of ritual purity.

Although North African amphorae dominate assemblages within the West Mediterranean, the 15 types recorded on Byzantine sites in Israel (Fig. 24, nos 2-3; Fig. 26, nos 1-2; Fig. 27, nos 2-3) have a highly restricted distribution. The two types of Egyptian amphora imported into Palestine during the Byzantine period, Egyptian Type A (Class 53 in Peacock and Williams 1986; Bailey, 1998; Fig. 24, no. 6) and LR7 (Fig. 24, no. 1), are equally rare, recorded on only two and four sites respectively. Far more prevalent were six eastern Mediterranean amphora types (Kingsley 1999a: 165-8): carrot-shaped amphorae from the southern Black Sea region (or possibly a Syrian imitation; Fig. 28, no. 5), MR4 (Fig. 26, no. 3), MR7 (Fig. 27, nos 4-5), LR1 (Fig. 23), LR2 (Fig. 24, nos 4-5) and LR3 (Fig. 25).

LR1 amphorae manufactured in North Syria, Cilicia, Cyprus and Rhodes (Empereur and Picon 1989; Demesticha and Michaelides 2001) were the most common amphora type imported into Byzantine Palestine. They occur on 60 sites and represent 44% of all imported eastern amphorae distributed throughout the province (and 33% of the total imported amphorae, based on site count). LR2 amphorae probably imported from Chios, Kounapi in the Greek Peloponnese and other sites

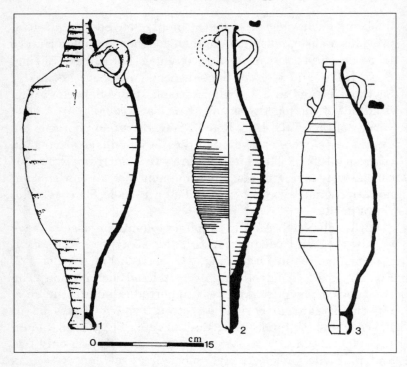

Fig. 25. Imported Byzantine amphorae found in Israel: LR3 (nos 1-2, Caesarea; no.3, Sumaqa). (After Oleson *et al.* 1994: fig. 34, A61; Siegelmann 1974: 220, no. 5; Kingsley 1999b: fig. 23, no. 25.)

near the Black Sea or the Aegean Sea (Arthur 1989: 82; Bonifay and Villedieu 1989: 25) have been recorded at 19 sites. The LR3 amphora imported from Asia Minor, probably from the vicinity of Halicarnassus or Sardis (Bonifay and Piéri 1995: 112), is the second most common non-local container found in Byzantine Palestine, excavated at 22 sites (Kingsley 1999a: 168).

Although imported amphorae had a very wide distribution within Byzantine Palestine, reflecting consumption on a broad hierarchy of site types, quantified pottery assemblages indicate

6. Exports, imports and the balance of trade

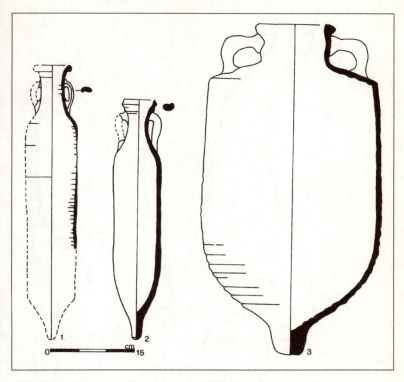

Fig. 26. Imported Byzantine amphorae found in Israel: Keay XXVE (no. 1, Ashkelon), Keay XXVG (no. 2, Shavei Zion), MR4 (no. 3, Jerusalem). (After Ronen and Zemer 1981: 50; Prausnitz 1967: fig. 11, no. 8; Hamilton 1944: 46, no. 6.)

that the scale of importation was low. LR1 is the most common import, representing between 0.1% and 6.0% of total amphora assemblages. Aegean LR2 amphorae represented less than 0.3% of all amphorae at the Caesarea hippodrome, at Sumaqa and Tel Fara. The figure of 3.9% in the Late Byzantine Building at Caesarea is the highest recorded frequency. Both one and two-handled LR3 amphorae occur inland in significant quantities in fourth- and early fifth-century contexts at Jalame (6.5%)

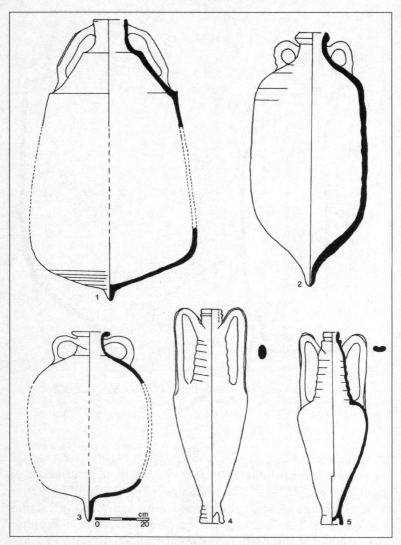

Fig. 27. Imported Byzantine amphorae found in Israel: HC1 (no. 1, Carmel Beach), Keay IIIB (no. 2, Sinai), Keay I (no. 3, Carmel Beach), MR7 (nos 4-5, Jerusalem and Rosh Ha'ayin). (After Raban 1969-71: 68; Ben-Arieh 1974: 93; Raban 1969-71: 68; Hamilton 1944: 46, no. 5; Eitan 1969: 65.)

6. Exports, imports and the balance of trade

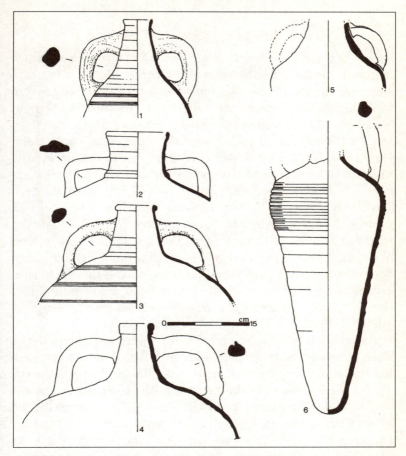

Fig. 28. Imported Byzantine amphorae found in Israel: Keay XCI (no. 1, Dor), SUM2 (no. 2, Dor), LR13 (nos 3-4, Dor and Caesarea), 'carrot' amphora (no. 5, Jalame), Beirut amphora (no. 6, Sumaqa). (After Kingsley and Raveh: 1996: fig. 35, P21; fig. 35, P26; fig. 35, P25; Oleson *et al.* 1994: fig. 5, A36; Johnson 1988: 213, no. 753; Kingsley 1999b: fig. 12, no. 26.)

and Sumaqa (6.1%), but after this date import declines and does not exceed 1.6% *c.* AD 630-60 at Caesarea (tabulated in Kingsley 1999a: 168-9).

Import markets: fine-wares

Owing to their conspicuous fabric and stamped surfaces, which facilitate simple identification, fine-wares offer a more conspicuous picture of the distribution of a type of import within the Holy Land. Fine-wares have been recorded throughout Israel on 179 sites located between Shelomi in the north of Israel, Dabiyye in the Golan to the east, and Wadi Umm Hashim in the Negev Desert (Fig. 29). This figure is twice as high as the number of sites where imported amphorae are registered. Phocaean Red Slip bowls (PRS) from western Turkey occur at 135 sites, Cypriot Red Slip (CRS) at 100, African Red Slip (ARS) at 72 sites, and Egyptian Red Slip (ERS) at 13 sites. Although only a few assemblages have been quantified, available evidence suggests that CRS may have been the dominant imported fine-ware during the Early Byzantine period, being replaced by PRS from the second half of the fifth century until the mid-seventh century (Kingsley 1999a: 170-1).

As with amphorae, imported bowls were not restricted to sites of specific status. Both PRS and CRS wares have each been recorded in 17 urban sites and ARS in 18 city contexts. These three types are known from 14, ten and six towns respectively. By contrast, in rural areas PRS occurs on 38 sites, CRS is known from 21 sites, and ARS from 11 sites. Imports are very common on Christian sites (PRS: 12 churches, 11 monasteries, two chapels, two pilgrimage holy sites) and are equally common on Jewish sites (CRS: seven synagogues and two Jewish villages). Most notable are the 755 fragments excavated from the synagogue and residential units in the remote Jewish village of Sumaqa in the Carmel from deposits dated to between the fourth and seventh centuries (Kingsley 1999b).

6. Exports, imports and the balance of trade

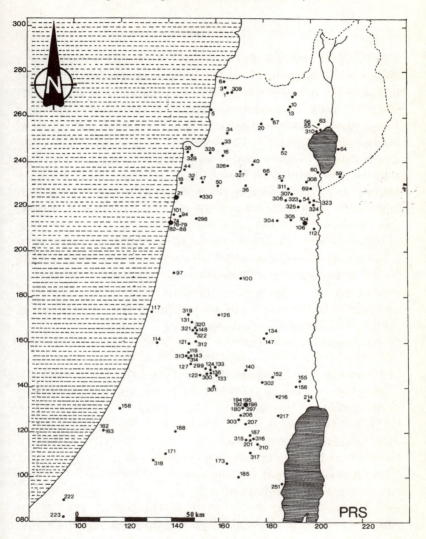

Fig. 29. Distribution map of Phocaean Red Slip (PRS) bowls imported into Byzantine Palestine from Asia Minor. (Numbers refer to catalogue nos in Kingsley 1999a: 301-40.)

Discussion

The ceramic evidence for booming Palestinian wine exports between *c.* AD 400 and 650 clearly indicates substantial capital investment and complex logistics in production and distribution. If Palestine was comparable to the structure of the wine industry recorded in Egyptian papyri (Kruit 1992: 275), then in many cases shipment orders will have been secured alongside guarantees of product quality even while grapes were still on the vine. The primitivist notion of a *laissez faire* society, where farmers cultivated crops and merchants randomly plied sea-lanes with little business acumen, pays Late Antiquity a serious injustice.

Nevertheless, the pattern and scale of Palestinian amphora distribution overseas provide no certainties about the specific economic rationale underlying wine shipments, so that interpretation of exchange structures will rarely proceed independently beyond mere probability theory. Six forms of exchange co-existed in Late Antiquity, but which models best fit Palestinian wine exports?

(i) Economic inter-dependence: export to regions where demographic pressure caused demand to exceed local production potential.
(ii) Harvest failure.
(iii) Ecclesiastical reciprocity.
(iv) State military taxation: *annona militaris*.
(v) State civic taxation: *annona civica*.
(vi) Commerce: open market trade.

Although Hopkins (1983b: 90) has argued that the first two categories above explain most bulk foodstuff export because 'Roman inter-town trade in staples was by and large a topping up operation, the satisfaction of a marginal demand, a transfer

6. Exports, imports and the balance of trade

of an occasional surplus to places where there was an unpredicted need', in reality the long-distance shipment of consumables would have been both unnecessarily time-consuming, expensive and inefficient. In ideal circumstances, city administrators would prefer to procure staple produce from the nearest geographical source. However, it is not inconceivable that this model may explain several anomalous, large concentrations of Palestinian amphorae such as the 44.7% of Palestinian amphorae in the Canadian excavations at Carthage (Hayes 1980: 205), the 43.2% of LR5 in Cistern D27 in the same city (Riley 1981: 90), and perhaps even Marseille La Bourse, where Palestinian amphorae represented 19.8% of all amphorae between the late sixth and first half of the seventh century (Bonifay 1986: 303-4).

Ecclesiastical reciprocity (non-monetary exchange conducted to maintain social and political alliances) is described in colourful detail in historical texts, not least gifts of timber discussed in letters between Gregory the Great and Eulogius of Alexandria by letter from AD 596 to 603 (Monks 1953: 356). Identifying such activity on the ground, however, to date has eluded archaeologists. Wine presses capable of processing surpluses have certainly been recorded in numerous monasteries and ecclesiastical properties across Israel, and it would be naïve to deny the existence of a steady stream of inter-community reciprocity between brethren. But any export is unlikely to have been especially significant to the mainstream provincial and political economy. (This does not exclude the certainty that the church was a prime mover in large-scale commercial maritime trade; cf. van Alfen 1996; Mundell Mango 2001.)

The aggregate food consumption demands of the Byzantine army exerted massive pressure on state revenues and thus on Byzantine farmers, who were taxed as a means of obtaining the *annona militaris*. Assessments of scales of this burden vary quite widely due to uncertainty about the changing size of the military machine over time. During the reign of Constantine I

(AD 307-37) the total size of the Byzantine army may have been around 645,000 soldiers (Treadgold 1995: 53), a figure that seems to have been reduced significantly under Justinian in the sixth century to about 150,000 soldiers (Whitby 1995: 73). (Agathias' omission of *limitanei* from this count, who may not have been retained as salaried soldiers during the reign of Justinian, may partly explain the difference in size between the fourth and sixth century figures, besides, of course, the loss of the West.)

In addition to a regular monetary *stipendium*, and annual donatives paid to troops on the birthday or accession date of an imperial patron, most scholars agree that soldiers were paid primarily (or at least substantially) in kind until at least the early fifth century (Segrè 1943: 406; Southern and Dixon 1996: 76, 81). Thus, in AD 393 an edict discussing *De Erogatione Militaris Annonae* in the Theodosian Code stated that 'No person shall attempt to demand money instead of subsistence allowances payable in kind' (*CTh*. 7.4.18; Pharr 1952: 16). The difficulties of preventing army units illegally over-taxing provincial populations, of fraudulent commutation, and of soldiers' preference for a monetary salary, seem to have resulted in an abandonment of the *annona militaris* procured and distributed in kind during the fifth century. Certainly a prohibition against exacting such payments was authorised in the Orient and Egypt in AD 409 (*CTh*. 17.4.30; Pharr 1952: 162). The benefits of levying in coin would have been primarily administrative, reducing the state's logistical need to manage bulk foodstuff transport overland and by ship.

Wine certainly was a staple ingredient of the *annona militaris*. In AD 398, an edict was passed to ensure that 'Your Illustrious Authority shall arrange that subsistence allowances of new wine shall be issued from the month of November to all the service units and soldiers throughout all the provinces' (*CTh*. 7.4.25; Pharr 1952: 161-2). A sixth-century Egyptian

6. Exports, imports and the balance of trade

papyrus (*P.Oxy.* 2046; Southern and Dixon 1996: 79) refers to peacetime military daily food rations consisting of the equivalent of 1.1 litres of wine alongside 1.4 kg of bread, 1.0 kg of meat and 0.07 litres of oil.

But since the commutation of military payments from kind to coin pre-dated the emergence of a developed Palestinian wine industry for the export market, there is little room to argue that the military *annona* had anything other than a minimal impact on stimulating this industry. In terms of long-distance trade this point is further compounded by the reality that essential food rations seem to have been purchased from sources as close as possible to military camps or forts (no doubt for logistical efficiency and to ensure product freshness). Edict 7.4.15 in the Theodosian Code, dated to AD 369, states that throughout the Empire 'Just as We, by Our beneficial foresight, have commanded to be done throughout all frontiers, you shall order supplies of subsistence allowances to be brought to the camps by the provincials nearest the borders' (Pharr 1952: 160). Thus, from the early fifth century Byzantine soldiers seem to have been abandoned to market forces in the procurement of rations.

Rome's *annona civica* policy, an early form of the Welfare State, was adopted in the Eastern Roman Empire in imitation of the Eternal City. According to John Malalas, in AD 330 Constantine 'distributed largesse in Constantinople to the [citizens of Byzantium]; these were reed tokens for perpetual daily bread distribution. He called the loaves 'palatine' because they were given out in the palace. He set aside wine, meat and garments with each loaf and set aside revenues for them from his own resources; he called the loaves "politikoi" (civil)' (*Chronicle* 13.322-3; Jeffreys *et al.* 1986: 175). Initially distributed to 80,000 recipients annually, the *annona* was reduced to less than 40,000 people during the reign of Constantius, between AD 337 and 360 (Sirks 1991b: 225). The scale of free wheat redistributions in the fifth and sixth centuries has been calculated at five million *modii* (Durliat 1990: 269), the equivalent of about 350,000 tons maximum, a large percentage of which was imported from Egypt, granary of the Eastern Roman Empire. Thus, perhaps some 624 state shipments of 50-ton capacity sailed past Palestine annually (Kingsley and Decker 2001: 2). Heraclius' capture of the grain fleet off Carthage in AD 610 *en route* to Constantinople, to feed his army during the rebellion against Phocas (Sirks 1991a: 166, n. 66), confirms that the *annona* infrastructure endured into the early seventh century. Historical sources also suggest that olive oil was a structured element of the *annona* supply to Constantinople (*CTh.* 14.17.15; Pharr 1952: 420).

Whether wine remained an integral component of the *annona civica* package is uncertain from historical sources, and the paucity of amphora assemblages examined from urban dumps in Constantinople, capital of the Eastern Late Roman Empire, leaves these waters particularly murky. The 3% of Palestinian amphorae excavated at Saraçhane (Hayes 1968: 215), however, does little to fuel speculation that the Holy Land was involved in this obligation. The very early deposition of 9% of Palestinian LR4 containers among amphorae recorded by the Aub-Leverhulme excavations at Beirut *c.* AD 325-50, doubling to 19% by *c.* AD 360-400 (Reynolds 1997-8: 54), is a fascinating anomaly. The urban development of Constantinople and flow of *annona civica* towards this great city may very well explain this deposition pattern. But for the fifth century there is no evidence that the state collected anything other than taxes in coin from the three provinces of Palestine, and certainly by AD 494/5 the procurement of taxes across the eastern Mediterranean was in any case commuted from kind to coin by decree of Anastasius I (*Malalas* 16.394; Jeffreys *et al.* 1986: 221).

Finally, what of entrepreneurial trade, so long the ugly stepsister of Byzantine history? Traditionally, the limited body of written texts describing commerce has been interpreted as

6. Exports, imports and the balance of trade

absence of activity. However, just as there is no doubt that in production and consumption the availability of *terra sigillata* in Roman markets was a commercial business, so similar forces were engrained in Late Roman and Byzantine society. After AD 395 the Roman Empire was politically divided into independent states and local aristocracies, which no longer shared economic resources; between 442 and 534 North Africa was also controlled by a hostile Vandal administration. As Ward-Perkins has argued (2000: 371), the 'pattern of exports within the West, before and after the collapse of Roman power, should therefore tell us whether the existence of state-mechanisms of distribution were essential for the distribution of goods over long distances'. The uninterrupted import of Palestinian amphorae to the West after the Empire was divided, discussed above, can simply only be explained in terms of open trade.

Semi-luxury, non-local foodstuffs clearly held great appeal for consumers, a fact reflected in grades of content, including 'top quality' written as advertising on the sides of several types of amphorae (Curtis 1984-6; Derda 1992: 138, 141). The presence of single Palestinian amphorae on the Byzantine shipwrecks Dramont E (Santamaria 1995: 63), Yassi Ada A (Bass 1982: 184, P 73) and Saint-Gervais 2 (Jézégou 1998: 345), as well as on land in the fort at Chios (Ballance *et al.* 1989: pl. 25) and a shop at Sardis (Stephens Crawford 1990: 97) are most rationally explained simply as examples of commercial trade in wine purchased for its semi-exotic value.

The absence of formal stamps and *tituli picti* on Palestinian amphorae, which were prominent on some Late Roman Tunisian amphorae as well as on LR1 and LR2 types (Fig. 23, nos 4, 6; Fig. 24, no. 4), is a further anomaly that may suggest less formal centralised state control over the wine trade. Such marks placed on Spanish and North African amphorae reflected estate ownership and government checks on weight and quality, and often identified the merchant responsible for overseas transport (Peacock and Williams 1986: 13-14; Tomber 1988a: 33). Their absence raises the distinct possibility that it was independent merchants, functioning as middlemen, who purchased Palestinian wine produced in numerous villages and farms for wholesale trade.

A final potent argument for the widespread existence of commercial trade in Palestinian wine during Late Antiquity is amphora imitation. Copies of bag-shaped LR5 containers were produced in Jordan, while those from Abu Mena (Empereur and Picon 1992: 150) and the Nile region (Bailey 1998: 137) were distributed throughout Egypt. Was the manufacture of such imitations possibly a marketing ploy conceived to exploit the special reputation of Holy Land wines, cultivated from soils where the Twelve Tribes of Israel and later Jesus and the Apostles trod? Very possibly so.

Within the web of exchange systems co-existing in the Late Antique eastern Mediterranean, commercial trade best fits current patterns of Palestinian wine exports. If this is the case, what kind of prosperity did such sea-trade bring to the Holy Land? Statistics derived from 12 quantified assemblages in Israel demonstrate that the lowest combined recorded level of Palestinian vessels among amphora assemblages is 68.5% at En Boqeq, a military fort in the Negev Desert. The highest level is a figure of 99% recorded at Ohad, a frontier town on the northern edge of the Negev Desert. The average presence of LR4 at Byzantine sites in Israel is just under 19% and the average LR5 figure just under 71%. In combination, Palestinian amphorae account for an average of 90% of all amphorae found on archaeological sites in Byzantine Palestine (Kingsley 1999a: 180).

Imported amphorae were easily accessible in Palestine during Late Antiquity, but although they were distributed as far as 85 km inland to the Negev Desert fort of Upper Zohar (Harper 1995: 31), the volume involved was unremarkable. The average

6. Exports, imports and the balance of trade

figures recorded are 4.1% for LR1, 0.5% for LR2, 1.2% for LR3, 0.3% for Beirut and Syrian carrot-shaped amphorae, 1.0% for Egyptian amphorae, and 0.2% for North African amphorae (Kingsley 1999a: 180). The dominant role of local amphorae and produce is not just restricted to the rural sector, where self-sufficiency would be expected. Three of the amphora assemblages quantified are from cities (Caesarea Hippodrome dump, Caesarea Late Byzantine Building, and Dor church). Both Caesarea and Dor possessed major Byzantine harbours (Oleson *et al.* 1994: 161; Kingsley and Raveh 1996: 82-5) and were located along the primary *annona civica* sea-lane linking Egypt with Constantinople. However, at Caesarea Palestinian amphorae accounted for 90% of all amphorae in the hippodrome deposit, 75% in the Late Byzantine Building, and 97% at Dor (Kingsley 1999a: 180). The reliance on Palestinian staple foodstuffs is an interesting pattern, which is very different to trends recorded in other Mediterranean regions (see below).

The geographical distribution of fine-ware bowls imported from western Asia Minor, Cyprus and North Africa is wider than for non-local amphorae. Imports were dominant among bowl assemblages recorded on all types of Byzantine sites in Israel dated between the mid-fifth and mid-seventh centuries. Both PRS and CRS were extremely common, while ARS usually did not exceed 17% of fine-ware assemblages. Egyptian products were rare throughout Late Antiquity until the Umayyad period, when they filled a void in supply. Palestinian pottery workshops seem not to have produced bowls on a significant scale and did not choose to compete commercially with imported fine-wares. Even during the second half of the fourth century, imports were considerably more prevalent than local wares in the agricultural and industrial estate at Jalame in the Galilee, where they accounted for 69% of all bowls (Johnson 1988: 146-67). Some Galilean products penetrated the markets of Caesarea and Scythopolis, but the majority of material circulated locally (Adan-Bayewitz 1993: fig. 11). By the first half of the fifth century, the already declining pottery workshops of Kfar Hananya apparently ceased production, effectively enabling imported fine-wares to monopolise Palestinian markets.

The pattern of amphorae distribution identified in Byzantine Palestine is dissimilar to that identified in other regions of the Mediterranean, where imports occur in large quantities in coastal towns. Thus, in pottery deposits examined in the northeast Tarraconensian towns of Barcino, Empuries, Rhodas, and Tarraco, Spanish containers represent on average only 8% of all amphorae during Late Antiquity, with 80% originating from Tunisia (Keay 1984). Similarly, in Italy imported amphorae of AD 350-480 at Naples account for 70% of all containers, and Italian amphorae recorded in the Temple of Magna Mater in Rome range from 7.8% to 17.5% maximum (Reynolds 1995: 184, 335). In France, imported amphorae constituted 97% of the total amphora assemblage in early fifth-century Arles, and between 71% and 77% at Marseille between AD 400 and 650/700 (Reynolds 1995: 184-5). Patterns identified in Carthage appear more complex. Up to c. 450, imports constituted no higher than 6.8% of all amphorae. However, between c. 450 and the seventh century, imported amphorae became extremely common, representing 15.2-35% of all amphorae. Throughout Late Antiquity, in some deposits at Carthage imports account for 40-65% of the total amphora assemblage (Reynolds 1995: 185-6). At Beirut imports account for 64% of all amphorae by the late fourth to early fifth century (Reynolds 1997-8: 51).

The low levels of amphorae imported into Byzantine Palestine fit the model of a province that was self-sufficient in agricultural produce. This seems to apply to wine, oil and, although incapable of proof using archaeology, also wheat. If olive oil was rare in Palestine, much higher levels of imported LR1 might be expected in the archaeological record. In any case the province's hundreds of oil presses leave no doubt of the

6. Exports, imports and the balance of trade

olive's omnipresence (Frankel 1999). The argument that the need for imported foodstuffs at coastal cities and towns during Late Antiquity was the rule, not the exception (Reynolds 1995: 123), seems applicable to the West but is invalid in the case of the Byzantine Holy Land.

Although taxation is often viewed as one of the evils of the age, restricting social mobility, pottery imports suggest that taxes were not so severe that the rural sector was unable to progress beyond simple subsistence farming. PRS, CRS and ARS fine-wares have been recorded throughout Byzantine Palestine, close to the coast and inland, in urban and rural contexts, and on settlements inhabited by people from different religious backgrounds. The most likely explanation for the presence of these imported wares on small rural settlements specialising in wine (and oil) production, is that they represent an archaeologically visible set of material culture reflecting profits from surplus crop sales. The few imported amphorae identified on numerous rural sites, apparently purchased for their prestige value and exotic taste, are a second possible indication of the profits obtained by peasant communities' trade in surplus crops. Imported pottery thus represents the only trace element surviving within the archaeological record of a far wider range of imports, long perished. As such, the humble sherd is the 'key witness' in the study of this long-distance trade.

Coins excavated in villages demonstrate that rural communities were monetised and participated in an open market. Excavations in the synagogue within the village of Qatzrin uncovered 180 coins dating between the reigns of Anastasius I and Phocas (AD 491-610; Ariel 1996). About 1,000 late sixth- and early seventh-century coins were recovered from a deposit located just outside the synagogue in the village of Korazin (ESI, 1984: 67). A hoard of 1,943 coins from the synagogue in the village at Gush Halav (Ariel 1987: 148) would have been collected in part from the local residents. About 458 coins were excavated from residential units and the synagogue in the Jewish village of Sumaqa in the Carmel, originating in Alexandria, Antioch, Aquileia, Carthage, Constantinople, Cyzicos, Heraclea, Nicomedia and Thessalonica (Kindler 1999).

The large-scale trade in ARS fine-wares throughout the western Mediterranean is broadly interpreted as a means by which merchants could profit from the state's *annona* shipments. Crates of fine-wares stowed in opportune spaces within a fiscal cargo, as a saleable space-filler, enabled merchants to impose a commercial trade network over the fiscal one (Wickham 1988: 191). The absence of pottery workshops specialising in fine-ware production in Byzantine Palestine is a possible indication that in this province sufficient profit was achievable through agricultural production and trade to prevent the local population competing in this market. In particular, the grape should be considered a highly profitable commercial crop. It is hard to believe that fine-wares manufactured in Jerusalem, and stamped with biblical characters or religious motifs, would not have found an eager overseas market at a time when Palestine was the 'flagship' of a Christian Empire.

The specific characteristics of surplus crop production, large-scale export, minimal import and prosperity in the rural sector, which typify the economy of the Byzantine Holy Land, also characterised the region in the late eighteenth and nineteenth centuries. As late as 1925 Palestine remained a rural society where 60% of its inhabitants worked in agriculture (Issawi 1982: 20). Although census figures indicate that in 1905 the country's population consisted of 763,600 inhabitants (Schnelz 1990: 67), somewhat lower than Broshi's estimate of one million for the Holy Land (1979: 3-5), Palestine was similarly self-sufficient in the provision of staple foodstuffs and produced surplus cash crops for export. These included watermelons

6. Exports, imports and the balance of trade

grown along the coastal fringe and in the Galilean valleys (Ben-Artzi 1990: 138).

The diversity of crops cultivated throughout the country also minimised the risk of famine and the need to import foodstuffs (Wilson 1906: 188). Statistics describing the average proportions of crop types under cultivation in North Palestine between 1858 and 1862 reflect the wide range of agricultural activities pursued: 40% wheat, 14% olives, 13% sesame, 9% barley, 7% dura, 6% cotton, 5% lentils, beans and peas, 4% water-melons, vineyards and figs, and 2% tobacco (Schölch 1982: 61). Similar conditions existed in the Late Antique Holy Land, when regional geographical diversity enabled different areas to feed others in times of low harvest yields.

Between 1856 and 1882 wheat from the Hauran, North Palestine and Gaza was exported by ship in large volumes to Italy, France, England, Greece, Lebanon and Asia Minor. In 1879, 1,750 tons left Palestinian ports. The average annual export figure from Jaffa between 1873 and 1882 was 10.04 million litres of wheat, 15.4 million litres from Haifa between 1872 and 1880, and 46.4 million litres from Akko between 1873 and 1880 (based on measurements given in *kiles* in Schölch 1982: 13, 57). Olive oil remained an essential export commodity into the nineteenth century, with 48.24 million litres exported from the ports of Acre, Haifa and Jaffa annually between 1872 and 1882 (Schölch 1982: 57). The absence of wine from this picture is due to general (but not total) abstention during the Islamic period, when grapes were cultivated mainly as a fruit for local consumption.

As in Byzantine Palestine, imports were considerably less numerous than exports during the nineteenth century. Between 1825 and 1826 produce valued at £2,834 entered Akko, whereas £13,036 worth of goods were exported from the port. In Haifa, between 1880 and 1881 the balance of import versus export was £9,946 against £74,430 (Kark 1990: 78-9). Thus, export was 4.5 times greater than import at Akko and 7.5 times at Haifa. The non-local commodities that entered the country consisted mainly of unavailable raw material for construction and semi-luxury foodstuffs.

A significant quantity of the produce cultivated was obtained by Ottoman land-owners through tax levied partly in kind. Taxation levels seem to have varied, but were typically a tenth of the total agricultural output cultivated between 1800 and 1914. In practice, they could vary from 10-50% (Owen 1981: 11) and as late as 1925 some farmers in Syria and Palestine paid 20%-22.5% of their produce, in lieu of tax and rent in coin (Issawi 1982: 20). However, the on-sale of goods levied in kind does not alone explain the high level of exports. In 1856, a foreign Consul in Palestine observed that a notable consequence of the agricultural export was that 'coin is poured in from abroad for payment. An Ionian merchant of Caiffa [Haifa] ... assures me that last year no less than half a million sterling passed through his hands between the ships of that port and the Bedaween of the Hauran, who have on their side imported no merchandise. It is the same with the peasantry of the villages, they export grain, they greedily grasp the coin in return, and then hide it in the ground often dying without revelation of their secret' (Schölch 1982: 18-19). While there is certainly no evidence of widespread hoarding in Byzantine Palestine, there is extensive evidence of spending power and of a balance of trade characterised by comparable large-scale exports and relatively low-level imports that brought generalised prosperity to a broad stratum of society.

7

Shipwreck archaeology: an integrated future

This debate into the interpretative parameters of shipwreck archaeology in the Holy Land has taken a circuitous route. The traditional argument denouncing the very existence of a maritime tradition in ancient Palestine and modern Israel has been abandoned in its wake; and the 'artificial economy' theory of the Byzantine economy has been proved unrealistically simplistic. It is clear that maritime trade touched far wider strata of society than history books currently relate and was not the exclusive domain of a coercive state and dominant church order.

One of the most important points to emerge is one of diversity: just like modern Jerusalem, Palestine's Byzantine society was one where rich and poor, Christian, Jewish, Samaritan and secular classes rubbed shoulders. State taxation was certainly an omnipresent, inescapable reality, but not one that crippled rural communities to the sole advantage of urban aristocrats and the social elite. Many of the Palestinian amphorae scattered across the Mediterranean may have been peddled by well-appointed middle-class merchants, but the wine within was processed predominantly by farmers, frequently independent operatives fully aware of the commercial appeal of their crop and, I would suggest, equally aware that surplus production could equal profit.

This is evident from the refuse fortuitously left behind for archaeologists on the floors of village houses at sites such as Sumaqa in the Carmel. The sherds of prestigious imported bowls and amphorae once containing semi-exotic oils, wines, honeys and fish sauces turn up alongside coins, indicative of a monetised society drawing together both town and country. Surely it was such coin that attracted merchants to the likes of the festival of St Sergius in the Byzantine city of Gaza, where booths were 'copiously laden with merchandise both for the rich and for those of moderate means', according to Choricius (*Laud. Marc.* 1.83; de Ligt 1993: 73).

Similar diverse social nuances emerge from the shipwrecks. Dor D's recycled amphorae and antiquated stone anchors are a far cry from the brand new cargo on board the Iskandil Burnu ship lying off Turkey, although both are broadly contemporary in date and operated within an identical Palestinian wine trade orbit. Meanwhile, as Dor D continued to rely on the tried and tested tenon-first shipbuilding technology, a new generation of merchants seems to have been speculating on more cheaply built ships, presumably to shave further costs off the expense of their trade. The 'feel' of the period apparent from the archaeological sources leans more towards 'modernistically mobile' than towards feudal medieval Europe.

Although our archaeological sources enable a new chapter to be opened in the social history of the Holy Land (for a period when business activity was largely inappropriate subject matter for contemporary commentators, as evident from the letters of Libanius of Antioch; Liebeschuetz 1972: 83), it is at the expense of historically attested state, church and Jewish exchange. This is a condition of archaeological visibility. Yet we are left to ponder just where are the hulls of the great merchant vessels that heaved wheat for redistribution as dole in Constantinople? How have the massive cargoes of metallic raw materials eluded us?

Returning to the myth of Jewish exclusion from maritime

7. Shipwreck archaeology: an integrated future

trade discussed in Chapter 2, the shipwreck archaeology sources currently offer no relief. Only in historical texts do lively accounts of Jewish seafaring emerge, including complex nautical terminology in the Talmud (Sperber 1986) and evidence of Jewish mariners and imported cargoes (Fitzgerald 1926: 80-7). Typical examples are rabbinical texts referring to ritually pure fish brine imported from Tyre to Roman Akko for Jewish consumption, and Rabbi Aba placing a guard around the ship to ensure that non-Jewish wine was not mixed with the cargo (Sperber 1970: 2, 11). While even some religious communities seem to have enjoyed imports, the Jewish inhabitants of villages like Sumaqa deliberately selected Cypriot and Turkish bowls for purposes of cultural identity and prestige, evidence of secular consumption. Again, only the enquiry of different sources reveals a realistic diversity of trade functions.

The database available is clearly far from representative of Late Antique exchange in its totality. Given this reality it seems incongruous that the discipline currently focuses so strongly on the complete excavation of individual ships, as if these can serve as missing links for the trade of entire periods. To assess the fluctuating histories of extensive landscapes, archaeology has a long and highly successful tradition of surface survey that enables soil exploitation to be linked to satellite villages, rural estates and the mother city politically dominating a region. A web of arterial data is analysed to reconstruct regional history. Why has a similar integrated concept not been initiated for shipwreck archaeology so that research strategies can address similar holistic questions? Why have no surveys tried to build on the rich sources available for Roman oil and grain export from North Africa to Rome (see Chapter 1) to tangibly discover how state and merchant interacted? Why has no Byzantinist addressed one of the most intellectually stimulating debates of Late Antiquity, the impact of the great Justinianic plague of AD 541 (alleged to have wiped out a third of the Mediterranean's population), by surveying a representative sample of East Mediterranean ships with a focus on cargo composition and site date? Such survey is proportionately far cheaper and logistically simpler to implement than full-scale shipwreck excavation, and the only reason for an absence of studies of this kind is a lack of analytical research ideas within the discipline.

For decades George Bass of the Institute of Nautical Archaeology at Texas A&M University has blazed a trail in establishing the foundations of shipwreck archaeology as a formal discipline. In a recent appraisal of the future of underwater archaeology (2002: 804) he wrote:

> I hope that our field does not remain in some academic minds outside the mainstream of archaeology. There are archaeologists who clearly do not read reports of ship excavations, no matter how important to their interests. Handbooks of Classical and Near Eastern archaeology still do not treat ships equally with architecture, coins, sculpture, and pottery, although ships were no less important to the ancients, and many of these ships are now as fully documented and published as sites on land. I hope that within a few decades we will all be known not as 'underwater archaeologists' but simply as the archaeologists we all are.

Professor Bass is, of course, quite right. From France to Turkey and Israel much outstanding research has been completed and published to standards that equal the finest excavations on land. The reason that Bass's shipwrecks are often marginalised, I suspect, is largely a matter of communication. Studies of nails and rotted hulls, in particular, are seen as areas of acute specialisation that tell us little about society in general, even though final reports published by Bass and his colleagues in-

7. Shipwreck archaeology: an integrated future

clude solid summaries that contextualise the archaeology. However, such work is almost always oriented from the maritime perspective rather than from that of the city, village, state, ecclesiastical order or merchant group that initiated a shipment. Further, such research may offer a brilliant view of one moment in time, but just how does one wreck fit into long-term history? As we have seen from the Holy Land, such shipwrecks often lend fascinating new primary data to models of trade and economies, but these subjects only truly come to life when contextualised with land-based archaeological and textual sources reflecting scales and structures of production and export. William Dever's argument in relation to Israel that 'The rarity of explicit and appropriate research designs has resulted in excavators not knowing how the mass of data that modern archaeology produces relates to significant issues ...' (1999: 15) is revealing in this regard.

Alongside the question of communication the failure of the Holy Land's shipwrecks to assume a more central stage within the mainstream discipline is without doubt the result of poor publication. Only in the mid-1990s have quality reports emerged, although the few detailed treatises available cover a minority of the total number of Byzantine shipwrecks recorded. An extensive mine of primary data currently languishes in the archives of the Israel Antiquities Authority, which has used the modern threat of treasure hunting and the corresponding necessity to combat this with rapid site recording to excuse simplistic, intuitive site sampling, low standards and limited publication.

In fairness this is hardly a dilemma confined to the maritime realm: the slow or non-appearance of final reports of surveys and excavations is currently the Achilles heel of archaeology in Israel in general, discussed in the two volumes on *Archaeology's Publication Problem* published by the Biblical Archaeology Society (Shanks 1996; 1999). As the inter-disciplinary character of excavation has increased since the 1960s, so the curve of publication has fallen. Never before has such success in teasing hard data from contexts existed. The modern site director's quandary is clear from statistics procured from a six-week season conducted at Tell Hazor in 1993, which employed about 80 workers and excavated 338 contexts, 20,000 sherds (of which about 1,000 needed drawing), 4,000 animal bones, 215 baskets of organic matter and 500 flints (Ben-Tor 1996: 34).

Ze'ev Herzog's assessment of historical rates of publication has demonstrated how full reports already appeared within two or three years of excavation in the late nineteenth and early twentieth centuries. Of the 107 excavation seasons conducted in Palestine between 1921 and 1939, 82% were fully published. From the 1940s onwards the large-scale annual sampling of huge Tell sites contributed to a regression. From the 1970s 33 of 44 sites remain unpublished. As Herzog summarises (1996: 100), 'It is important to emphasize that this problem is more serious in archaeology than in other sciences. The gravity of the situation stems from the unique nature of archaeology ... a one-time act .... This constraint underscores the need for full documentation and reminds us of the damage caused by the lack of publication.'

Although the sampling of shipwrecks off Israel produces far less primary data than Tell sites (but of relative greater potential quality), rates of both preliminary and full publication are nevertheless poor. Of the 200 shipwrecks recorded, only three final reports have materialised: the Atlit Hellenistic bronze warship's ram and timbers (Casson and Steffy 1991), the late first-century BC merchant vessel off north Caesarea (Fitzgerald 1994) and the sixth-century AD Dor D shipwreck (Kingsley 2002). Volume 1 of the late fifth-century BC Ma'agan Michael wreck report is currently in press. Thus only 4% of the country's recorded shipwreck heritage is available for study.

Sites excavated in Dor harbour since the 1990s have resulted

7. Shipwreck archaeology: an integrated future

in many outstanding preliminary reports, but fieldwork conducted between the 1960s and 1980s is poorly represented. Most of this work was directed by inspectors of the Israel Antiquities Authority, an organisation that has found the management of publishing its huge archive containing the results of thousands of excavations a labyrinthine challenge. In the case of marine archaeology, whatever happened to reports on the recovery of a Late Bronze Age cargo (fourteenth to thirteenth centuries BC) off Hahotrim in 1980 or of Hellenistic and Mamluk wreckage discovered off Megadim in 1982 containing important cargoes of coins, bronze statue parts, lighting devices and ingots? Extracting useful data from snippets of information published about Byzantine wreckage is a frustrating process (see Chapter 4), and non-publication continues to retard the development of the discipline. In terms of the unavailability of primary data capable of rewriting history, marine archaeology's non-publication issue in Israel is far worse than the infamous non-publication scandal surrounding the Dead Sea Scrolls. Although much IAA wreck survey work is defined as rescue archaeology, technically it is not, and certainly this should not excuse archaeologists from their duty to make results accessible to fellow scholars.

So what does the future hold? Certainly the quality of data from Israel's shipwrecks will be enhanced in the near future by the study of deepwater sites. As I write a research vessel is anchored over a mid-eighth-century BC Phoenician shipwreck that foundered off Ashkelon at a depth of 400 m. Deepwater shipwrecks offer remarkable preservation and intact cargoes, and advances in side-scan sonar and Remotely Operated Vehicle technology (ROVs) have made site identification and recording in the abyss a reality. As costs of this technology and exploration reduce, and science adapts to the massive potential of these sites as the future of the discipline, our understanding of the shipwreck archaeology of the Holy Land will be revolutionised. May that day arrive soon! Yet even then, if 'marine archaeologists' wish to propel their sources into the heart of mainstream studies, they ignore the reality that ships never sailed within cultural vacuums at their peril. The results obtained and their absorption into history books depends ultimately on the questions we demand of the data.

Bibliography

AJA = *American Journal of Archaeology*
ADAJ = *Annual of the Department of Antiquities of Jordan*
BAIAS = *Bulletin of the Anglo-Israel Archaeological Society*
BASOR = *Bulletin of the American School of Oriental Research*
CCE = *Cahiers de la Céramique Égyptienne*
CDS = *Cahiers d'Archéologie Subaquatique*
CEDAC = *Centre d'Études et de Documentation Archéologique de la Conservation de Carthage*
CMS News = *Center for Maritime Studies News*
DOP = *Dumbarton Oaks Papers*
ESI = *Excavations and Surveys in Israel*
IEJ = *Israel Exploration Journal*
IJNA = *International Journal of Nautical Archaeology*
INA Quarterly = *Institute for Nautical Archaeology Quarterly*
JRA = *Journal of Roman Archaeology*
PBSR = *Papers of the British School at Rome*
PEQ = *Palestine Exploration Quarterly*
RAN = *Revue Archéologique de Narbonnaise*
RDAC = *Report of the Department of Antiquities in Cyprus*
RIMS News = *Recanati Institute for Maritime Studies News*

Abadie, C., 1989. 'Les amphores protobyzantines d'Argos (IVe-VIe siècles)'. In V. Déroche and J.-M. Spieser (eds), *Recherches sur la céramique byzantine* (BCH Suppl. 18, Paris), 47-56.

Adan-Bayewitz, D., 1986. 'The pottery from the Late Byzantine Building and its implications (Stratum 4)'. In L.I. Levine and E. Netzer (eds), *Excavations at Caesarea Maritima 1975, 1976, 1979 – Final Report* (Qedem 21, Jerusalem), 90-129.

Adan-Bayewitz, D., 1993. *Common Pottery in Roman Galilee. A Study of Local Trade* (Ramat-Gan).

Amit, D., 1991. 'Khirbet Dah-Dah'. *ESI* 9, 162-3.

Bibliography

Amit, D., 1992. 'Khirbet Hilal'. *ESI* 10, 150-1.

Ariel, D.T., 1987. 'Coins from the synagogue at 'En Nashut'. *IEJ* 37, 147-57.

Ariel, D.T., 1996. 'A hoard of Byzantine folles from Qazrin'. *'Atiqot* 29, 69-76.

Arthur, P., 1985. 'Naples: notes on the economy of a Dark Age city'. In C. Malone and S. Stoddart (eds), *Papers in Italian Archaeology. Part IV. Classical and Medieval Archaeology* (BAR Int. S246), 247-60.

Arthur, P., 1989. 'Aspects of Byzantine economy: an evaluation of amphora evidence from Italy'. In V. Déroche and J.-M. Spieser (eds), *Recherches sur la céramique byzantine* (BCH Suppl. 18, Paris), 79-93.

Ashburner, W., 1909. *The Rhodian Sea-Law* (Oxford).

Atik, N., 1995. *Die keramik aus den südthermen von Perge* (Tübingen).

Avi-Yonah, M., 1958. 'The economics of Byzantine Palestine'. *IEJ* 8, 39-51.

Avi-Yonah, M., 1962. 'Scythopolis'. *IEJ* 12, 123-34.

Ayalon, E., Matthews, E. and Neidinger, W., 1994. 'Introduction to the excavations at Zur Natan'. In *Publication of the Texas Foundation for Archaeological and Historical Research* (Houston), 2-3.

Bagnall, R.S., 1993. *Egypt in Late Antiquity* (Princeton).

Bailey, D.M., 1998. *Excavations at El-Ashmunein V. Pottery, Lamps and Glass of the Late Roman and Early Arab Periods* (London).

Bakirtzis, C., 1996. 'Description and metrology of some clay vessels from Agios Georgios, Pegeia'. In V. Karageorghis and D. des Michaeli (eds), *The Development of the Cypriot Economy* (Nicosia), 153-60.

Ballance, M., Boardman, J., Corbett, S. and Hood, S., 1989. *Excavations in Chios 1952-1955. Byzantine Emporio* (BSA Suppl. 20, London).

Ballard, R.D., Hiebert, F.T., Coleman, D.E., Ward, C., Smith, J.S., Willis, K., Foley, B., Croff, K., Major, C. and Torre, F., 2001. 'Deepwater archaeology of the Black Sea: the 2000 season at Sinop, Turkey'. *AJA* 105, 607-23.

Ballard, R.D., Stager, L.E., Master, D., Yoerger, D., Mindell, D., Whitcomb, L.L., Singh, H. and Piechota, D., 2002. 'Iron Age shipwrecks in deep water off Ashkelon, Israel'. *AJA* 106, 151-68.

Barag, D., 1963. 'A survey of pottery recovered from the sea off the coast of Israel'. *IEJ* 13, 13-19.

Bascom, W., 1987. 'Deepwater salvage and archaeology'. In P. Throckmorton (ed.), *History from the Sea. Shipwrecks and Archaeology* (London), 222-5.

Bass, G.F., 1982. 'The pottery'. In G.F. Bass and F.H. van Doorninck (eds), *Yassi Ada I. A Seventh Century Byzantine Shipwreck* (Texas), 155-88

Bass, G.F., 1983. 'A plea for historical particularism in nautical archaeology'. In R.A. Gould (ed.), *Shipwreck Archaeology* (New Mexico), 91-104.

Bass, G.F, 1991. 'Evidence of trade from Bronze Age shipwrecks'. In N.H. Gale (ed.), *Bronze Age Trade in the Mediterranean* (Studies in Mediterranean Archaeology vol. XC, Goteborg), 68-92.

Bass, G.F., 2002. 'Archaeology in the 21st century'. In Carol V. Ruppé and Janet F. Barstad (eds), *International Handbook of Underwater Archaeology* (New York), 803-6.

Ben-Arieh, S., 1974. 'Survey between Raphia and the Brook of Egypt'. *'Atiqot* 7, 14.

Ben-Artzi, Y., 1990. 'Changes in the agricultural sector of the Moshavot, 1882-1914'. In G.G. Gilbar (ed.), *Ottoman Palestine 1800-1914. Studies in Economic and Social History* (Leiden), 131-58.

Ben David, H., 1998. 'Oil presses and oil production in the Golan in the Mishnaic and Talmudic periods'. *'Atiqot* 34, 1-61. (Hebrew.)

Ben-Tor, A., 1996. 'Why publication takes so long'. In H. Shanks (ed.), *Archaeology's Publication Problem* (Washington), 33-6.

Bien, S., 1998. 'Contextes de l'antiquité tardive sur le chantier du Parc des Phocéens (ilot 24 N)'. In M. Bonifay, M.-B. Carre and Y. Rigoir (ed.), *Fouilles à Marseille. Les mobiliers (Ier-VIIe siècles ap. J.-C.)* (Études Massaliètes, Paris), 275-83.

Bjelajac, L., 1996. *Amphoras of the Danubian Basin in Upper Moesia* (Belgrade).

Boardman, J., 1989. 'The finds'. In M. Ballance, J. Boardman, S. Corbett and S. Hood, *Excavations in Chios 1952-1955. Byzantine Emporio* (BSA Suppl. 20, London), 86-142.

Bonifay, M., 1986. 'Observations sur les amphores tardives à Marseille d'après les fouilles de la Bourse (1980-1984)'. *RAN* 19, 269-305.

Bonifay, M. and Piéri, D., 1995. 'Amphores du Ve au VIIe s. à Marseille: nouvelles données sur la typologie et le contenu'. *JRA* 8, 94-120.

Bonifay, M. and Villedieu, F., 1989. 'Importations d'amphores orientales en Gaule (V^e-VIIe siècle)'. In V. Déroche and J.-M. Spieser (eds), *Recherches sur la céramique byzantine* (BCH Suppl. 18, Paris), 17-46.

Brill, R.H., 1965. 'Beth She'arim'. *IEJ* 15, 261-2.

Bibliography

Broshi, M., 1979. 'The population of Western Palestine in the Roman-Byzantine period'. *BASOR* 236, 1-10.

Broshi, M., 1984. 'Wine in Ancient Palestine – introductory notes'. *Israel Museum Journal* 3, 21-40.

Broshi, M., 1986. 'The diet of Palestine in the Roman period – introductory notes'. *Israel Museum Journal* 5, 41-56.

Buckingham, J.S., 1821. *Travels in Palestine* (London).

Carignani, A. and Pacetti, F., 1989. 'Le importazioni di anfore Bizantine a Roma fra IV e V secolo: le evidenze di alcuni contesti ribani'. In V. Déroche and J.-M. Spieser (ed.), *Recherches sur la céramique Byzantine* (BCH Suppl. 18, Paris), 6-10.

Carmel, Z., Inman, D.L. and Golik, A., 1984. 'Transport of Nile sand along the southeastern Mediterranean coast'. In *The 19th Coastal Engineering Conference Proceedings, ASCE* (Houston), 1282-91.

Carmel, Z., Inman, D.L. and Golik, A., 1985. 'Characteristics of storm waves off the Mediterranean coast of Israel'. *Coastal Engineering* 9, 1-19.

Carmi, Y. and Segal, D., 1995. 'How old is the shipwreck from Tantura lagoon? The radiocarbon evidence'. *The INA Quarterly* 22, 12.

Casson, L., 1980. 'The role of the state in Rome's grain trade'. In J.H. d'Arms and E.C. Kopff (eds), *The Seaborne Commerce of Ancient Rome: Studies in Archaeology and History* (Rome), 21-34.

Casson, L. and Steffy, J.R., 1991. *The Athlit Ram* (Texas).

Clifton, C., 1896. *Saewulf (1102-1103 AD)* (Palestine Pilgrims Text Society, London).

[CMS News], 1988. 'Ashkelon Yam'. *CMS News* 15.

Congès, G. and Leguilloux, M., 1991. 'Un dépotoir de l'antiquité tardive dans le quartier de l'Esplanade à Arles'. *RAN* 24, 201-34.

Crowfoot, J.W. and Fitzgerald, G.M., 1927. *Excavations in the Tyropoeon Valley, Jerusalem 1927* (Annual of the Palestine Exploration Fund 5, London).

Cunningham Geikie, D.D., 1887. *The Holy Land and the Bible* (London).

Cuomo, J.-P. and Gassend, J.-M., 1982. 'La construction alternée des navires antiques et l'épave de la Bourse à Marseille'. *RAN* 15, 263-72.

Curtis, R.I., 1984-86. 'Product identification and advertising on Roman commercial amphorae'. *Ancient Society* 15-17, 209-28.

Dar, S., 1986. *Landscape and Pattern. An Archaeological Survey of Samaria 800 BCE – 636 CE* (BAR Int. Series 308, Oxford).

Dar, S., 1995. 'Food and archaeology in Romano-Byzantine Palestine'.

In J. Wilkins, M.J. Dobson and F.D. Harvey (eds), *Food in Antiquity* (Exeter), 326-35.

Dar, S., 1999. *Sumaqa. A Roman and Byzantine Jewish Village on Mount Carmel, Israel* (BAR Int. Series 815, Oxford).

Dauphin, C., 1998. *La Palestine Byzantine. Peuplement et populations*, vols I-III (BAR Int. Series 726, Oxford).

Demesticha, S. and Michaelides, D., 2001. 'The excavation of a Late Roman 1 kiln in Paphos'. In E. Villeneuve and P.M. Watson (eds), *La céramique byzantine et proto-Islamique en Syrie-Jordanie (IVe-VIIe siècles apr. J.-C.)* (Beirut), 289-96.

Derda, T., 1992. 'Inscriptions with the formula "God's Grace [is] a Gain" on Late Roman amphorae'. *ZPE* 94, 135-52.

Dever, W.G., 1999. 'Making final publication reports useful'. In H. Shanks (ed.), *Archaeology's Publication Problem*, vol. 2 (Washington), 15-28.

Dothan, M. and Freedman, D.N., 1967. *Ashdod I. The First Season of Excavations 1962* ('Atiqot, Jerusalem).

Durliat, J., 1990. *De la ville antique à la ville byzantine. Le problème des subsistances* (École Française de Rome, Rome).

Edgerton, H.E., Linder, E. and Tur-Caspa, Y., 1980. *Side Scan Sonar Survey for Ancient Wrecks along the Israeli Mediterranean Coast – November 1978* (Research Report No.1, Haifa).

Eitan, E., 1969. 'Excavations at the foot of Tel Rosh Ha'ayin'. *'Atiqot* 5, 6-7. (Hebrew.)

Emery, K.O. and Neev, D., 1960. 'Mediterranean beaches of Israel'. *Bulletin of the Geological Survey of Israel* 26, 1-20.

Empereur, J.-Y. and Picon, M., 1989. 'Les régions de production d'amphores impériales en Méditerranée orientale'. In *Amphores Romaines et histoire économique: dix ans de recherche* (Ecole Française de Rome, Rome), 223-48.

Empereur, J-Y. and Picon, M., 1992. 'La reconnaissance des productions des ateliers céramiques: l'exemple de la Maréotide'. *CCE* 3, 3-92.

[ESI], 1984. 'Korazin'. *ESI* 1, 64-7.

Eyben, E., 1980-1. 'Family planning in Graeco-Roman antiquity'. *Ancient Society* 11-12, 5-82.

Fischer, M., 1994. 'Horvat Zikhrin – 1987/1989'. *ESI* 12, 40-4.

Fitzgerald, A., 1926. *The Letters of Synesius of Cyrene* (Oxford).

Fitzgerald, G.M., 1931. *Beth-Shan Excavations 1921-1923. The Arab and Byzantine Levels*, vol. III (Philadelphia).

Fitzgerald, M.A., 1994. 'The ship'. In J.P. Oleson, M.A. Fitzgerald,

Bibliography

A.N. Sherwood and S.E. Sidebotham, *The Harbours of Caesarea Maritima. Results of the Caesarea Ancient Harbour Excavation Project 1980-85* (BAR Int. Series 594, Oxford), 163-223.

Flinder, A., Linder, E. and Hall, E.T., 1993. 'Survey of the ancient harbour of Akko, 1964-1966'. In M. Heltzer, A. Segal and D. Kaufman (eds), *Studies in the Archaeology and History of Ancient Israel* (Haifa), 199-225.

Foerster, G. and Tsafrir, Y., 1993. 'The Bet She'an excavation project (1989-1991). City Center (North)'. *ESI* 11, 3-12.

Frankel, R., 1999. *Wine and Oil Production in Antiquity in Israel and other Mediterranean Countries* (Sheffield).

Freed, J., 1993a. 'Pottery from *Sondage* 1'. In S.T. Stevens (ed.), *Bir el Knissia at Carthage: a Rediscovered Cemetery Church. Report No. 1* (JRA Suppl. 7, Michigan), 73-90.

Freed, J., 1994b. 'Pottery'. In A.M. Small and R.J. Buck (eds), *The Excavations of San Giovanni di Ruoti*. Vol. I: *The Villas and their Environment* (Toronto), 102-6.

Frier, B., 1982. 'Roman life expectancy: Ulpian's evidence'. *Harvard Studies in Classical Philology* 86, 213-51.

Fritsch, C. and Ben-Dor, I., 1961. 'The Link expedition to Israel, 1960'. *Biblical Archaeologist* 24, 50-9.

Fritz, V. and Kempinski, A., 1983. *Ergebnisse der Ausgrabungen auf der Hirbet el-Msas (Tel Masos) 1972-1975*. Teil II: *Tafelband* (Wiesbaden).

Galili, E., 1992. 'Navigation and commerce along the Israeli coast in Antiquity: finds from underwater surveys'. In *The Maritime Holy Land. Mediterranean Civilizations in Ancient Israel from the Bronze Age to the Crusades* (Haifa), 23-30.

Galili, E., Dahari, U. and Sharvit, J., 1993. 'Underwater surveys and rescue excavations along the Israeli coast'. *IJNA* 22, 61-77.

Galili, E. and Sharvit, J., 1992. 'Classification of underwater archaeological sites along the Mediterranean coast of Israel: finds from underwater and coastal archaeological research'. *Thracia Pontica* 5, 269-96.

Galili, E. and Sharvit, Y., 1999. 'Underwater surveys in the Mediterranean 1992-1996'. *ESI* 19, 96-101.

Galili, E., Sharvit, J. and Dahari, U., 2001. 'Ashqelon and the sea in light of the underwater and coastal archaeological findings'. In A. Sasson, Z. Safrai and N. Sagiv (eds), *Ashkelon. A City on the Seashore* (Tel Aviv), 11-38. (Hebrew.)

Bibliography

Garbsch, J., 1988. 'Wagen oder Waagen?'. *Bayerische Vorgeschichtsblatter* 53, 191-222.

Garnsey, P., 1998. *Cities, Peasants and Food in Classical Antiquity. Essays in Classical Antiquity* (Cambridge).

Gibbins, D.J.L., 1989. 'The Roman wreck of c. AD 200 at Plemmirio, near Siracusa (Sicily): second interim report. The domestic assemblage 1: medical equipment and pottery lamps'. *IJNA* 18, 1-25.

Gibson, S., 1995. *Landscape Archaeology and Ancient Agricultural Field Systems in Palestine* (PhD thesis, University College London).

Gichon, M., 1993. *En Boqeq. Ausgrabungen in Einer Oase am Toten Meer*, Band 1 (Mainz am Rhein).

Gill, M.V., 1986. 'The small finds'. In R.M. Harrison, *Excavations at Saraçhane in Istanbul*, vol. 1 (Princeton).

Gophna, R. and Ayalon, E., 1989. 'History of settlement in the Tel Michal region'. In Z. Herzog, G. Rapp and O. Negbi (eds), *Excavations at Tel Michal, Israel* (Minneapolis), 16-28.

Gorin-Rosen, Y., 1995. 'Hadera, Bet Eli'ezer'. *ESI* 13, 42-3.

Gorin-Rosen, Y., 2002. 'The Ancient glass industry in Eretz Israel – a brief summary'. *Michmanim* 16, 7-18.

Gorin-Rosen, Y. and Stern, E.J., 1995. 'Horvat Qav'. *ESI* 13, 17-18.

Grossmann, E., 1995. *Maritime Investigation of Tel-Michal and Apollonia Sites* (PhD thesis, Macquarie University).

Grosmann, E., 2001. *Maritime Tel Michal and Apollonia. Results of the Underwater Survey 1989-1996* (BAR Int. Series 915, Oxford).

Gutwein, K.C., 1981. *Third Palestine. A Regional Study in Byzantine Urbanization* (Washington).

Haldane, D., 1985. 'The 7th-century Yassi Ada ship anchors'. *INA Newsletter* 12, 6-7.

Hamilton, R.W., 1944. 'Excavations against the North Wall of Jerusalem'. *QDAP* 10, 1-54.

Harper, R.P., 1995. *Upper Zohar. An Early Byzantine Fort in Palaestina Tertia. Final Report of Excavations in 1985-1986* (BSAJ, Oxford).

Harrison, R., 2003. 'Creating the *Mary Rose* Tudor Ship Museum'. In P. Marsden, *Sealed by Time. The Loss and Recovery of the* Mary Rose (Portsmouth), 60-8.

Hayes, J.W., 1968. 'A seventh century pottery group'. *DOP* 22, 203-16.

Hayes, J.W., 1978. 'Pottery report – 1976'. In J.H. Humphrey (ed.), *Excavations at Carthage 1976 Conducted by the University of Michigan* (Michigan), 23-98.

Hayes, J.W., 1980. 'Late Roman pottery: a fifth-century deposit from

Bibliography

Carthage. Summary of amphorae types: 1M7'. *Antiquités Africaines* 16, 205.

Hayes, J.W., 1992. *Excavations at Saraçhane in Istanbul.* Vol. 2: *The Pottery* (Princeton).

Herzog, Z., 1996. 'With time, we're getting worse'. In H. Shanks (ed.), *Archaeology's Publication Problem* (Washington), 87-110.

Hirschfeld, Y., 1997. 'Farms and villages in Byzantine Palestine'. *DOP* 51, 33-71.

Hirschfeld, Y., 1998. 'Tel Shiqmona – 1994'. *ESI* 18, 19-20.

Hirschfeld, Y., 1992. *The Judean Monasteries in the Byzantine Period* (New Haven).

Hocker, F., 1995. 'Lead hull sheathing in Antiquity'. In H. Tzalas (ed.) *3rd International Symposium on Ship Construction in Antiquity, Tropis III* (Thessaloniki), 197-206.

Hocker, F.M. and Scafuri, M.P., 1996. 'The Bozburun Byzantine shipwreck excavation: 1996 campaign'. *INA Quarterly* 23, 3-9.

Holladay, J.S., 1982. *Cities of the Delta.* Part III: *Tell El-Maskhuta. Preliminary Report on the Wadi Tumilat Project 1978-1979* (Malibu).

Hopkins, K., 1983a. 'Introduction'. In P. Garnsey, K. Hopkins and C.R. Whittaker (eds), *Trade in the Ancient Economy* (London), ix-xxv.

Hopkins, K., 1983b. 'Models, ships and staples'. In P. Garnsey and C.R. Whittaker (eds), *Trade and Famine in Classical Antiquity* (Cambridge), 84-109.

Houston, G.W., 1988. 'Ports in perspective: some comparative materials on Roman merchant ships and ports'. *AJA* 92, 553-64.

Israel, Y., 1995. 'Survey of pottery workshops, Nahal Lakhish-Nahal Besor'. *ESI* 13, 106-7.

Issawi, C., 1982. *The Economic History of the Middle East and N. Africa* (London).

Jeffreys, E., Jeffreys, N. and Scott, R., 1986. *The Chronicle of John Malalas* (Melbourne).

Jézégou, M.-P., 1989. 'L'épave II de l'anse Saint-Gervais à Fos-sur-Mer (Bouches-du-Rhone): un navire du haut moyen-âge construit sur squelette'. In H. Tzalas (ed.), *First International Symposium on Ship Construction in Antiquity, Proceedings* (Piraeus), 139-46.

Jézégou, M.-P., 1998. 'Le mobilier de l'épave Saint-Gervais 2 (VIIe s.) à Fos-sur-Mer (B.-du-Rh)'. In M. Bonifay, M.-B. Carre and Y. Rigoir (eds), *Fouilles à Marseille. Les mobiliers (Ier-VIIe siècles ap. J.-C.)* (Études Massaliètes, Paris), 343-52.

Johnson, B.L., 1986. 'Syro-Palestinian bag-shaped amphoras in the

Bibliography

Athenian Agora and Corinth collections'. In J.-Y. Empereur and Y. Garlan (eds), *Recherches sur les amphores Grècques* (BCH Suppl. 13), 589-97.

Johnson, B.L., 1988. 'The pottery'. In G.D. Weinberg (ed.), *Excavations at Jalame* (Columbia), 137-226.

Johnson, B.L. and Stager, L.E., 1995. 'Ashkelon: wine emporium of the Holy Land'. In S. Gitin (ed.), *Recent Excavations in Israel* (Boston), 95-109.

Joncheray, J.-P., 1975. 'Une épave du bas-empire: Dramont F'. *CDS* 4, 91-132.

Joncheray, J.-P., 1997. 'Deux épaves du bas-empire romain. Deuxième partie: l'épave Héliopolis 1'. *CDS* 13, 137-64.

Jones, A.H.M., 1964. *The Later Roman Empire 284-602*, vol. II (Oxford).

Jones, A.H.M., 1974. *The Roman Economy* (Oxford).

Kahanov, Y., 2002-3. 'Dor (Tantura) 2002 Season'. *RIMS Newsletter* 29, 15.

Kahanov, Y. and Royal, J.G., 1996. 'The 1995 INA/CMS *Tantura A* Byzantine shipwreck excavation – hull construction report'. *CMS News* 23, 21-3

Kapitän, H., 1969. 'The church wreck off Marzamemi'. *Archaeology* 22, 122-33.

Kark, R., 1990. 'The rise and decline of the coastal towns in Palestine'. In G.G. Gilbar (ed.), *Ottoman Palestine 1800-1914. Studies in Economic and Social History* (Leiden), 69-89.

Karmon, N., 1992. 'The purple dye industry in Antiquity'. In *The Maritime Holy Land. Mediterranean Civilizations in Ancient Israel from the Bronze Age to the Crusades* (Haifa), 55-9.

Karmon, N. and Spanier, E., 1988. 'Remains of a purple dye industry found at Tel Shiqmona'. *IEJ* 38, 184-6.

Katsev, S.D., 1982. 'Miscellaneous finds'. In G.F. Bass and F.H. van Doorninck (ed.), *Yassi Ada I. A Seventh-Century Byzantine Shipwreck* (Texas), 266-95.

Keay, S.J., 1984. *Late Roman Amphorae in the Western Mediterranean. A Typology and Economic Study: the Catalan Evidence* (BAR Int. Series 196, Oxford).

Kennedy, H., 1985. 'From polis to madina: urban change in Late Antique and Early Islamic Syria'. *Past and Present* 106, 3-27.

Kindler, A., 1999. 'Summary of twelve years of numismatic finds in the excavations of Sumaqa (1983-1995)'. In S. Dar, *Sumaqa. A Roman and Byzantine Jewish Village on Mount Carmel, Israel* (BAR Int. Series 815, Oxford).

Kingsley, S., 1994-5. 'Bag-shaped amphorae and Byzantine trade: expanding horizons'. *BAIAS* 14, 39-56.

Kingsley, S., 1999a. *Specialized Production and Long-Distance Trade in Byzantine Palestine* (DPhil thesis, University of Oxford).

Kingsley, S., 1999b. 'The Sumaqa pottery assemblage: classification and quantification'. In S. Dar, *Sumaqa. A Roman and Byzantine Jewish Village on Mount Carmel, Israel* (BAR Int. Series 815, Oxford), 263-330.

Kingsley S., 2001. 'The economic impact of the Palestinian wine trade in Late Antiquity'. In S. Kingsley and M. Decker (ed.), *Economy and Exchange in the East Mediterranean during Late Antiquity* (Oxford), 44-68.

Kingsley, S., 2002. *A Sixth-Century AD Shipwreck off the Carmel Coast, Israel. Dor D and Holy Land Wine Trade* (BAR Int. Series 1065, Oxford).

Kingsley, S. and Decker, M., 2001. 'New Rome, new theories on inter-regional exchange. An introduction to the East Mediterranean economy in Late Antiquity'. In S. Kingsley and M. Decker (ed.), *Economy and Exchange in the East Mediterranean during Late Antiquity* (Oxford), 1-27.

Kingsley, S.A. and Raveh, K., 1994. 'Stone anchors from Byzantine contexts in Dor Harbour, Israel'. *IJNA* 23, 1-12.

Kingsley, S. and Raveh, K., 1996. *The Ancient Harbour and Anchorage at Dor, Israel. Results of the Underwater Surveys, 1976-1991* (BAR Int. Series 626, Oxford).

Kirwin, L.P., 1938. 'The pottery'. In. W.B. Emery, *The Royal Tombs of Ballana and Qustul* (Cairo), 386-99.

Kruit, N., 1992. 'The meaning of various words related to wine'. *ZPE* 90, 265-76.

Labat, J.-B., 1717. *Mémoires du Chevalier d'Arvieux, envoye extraordinaire du Roy à la porte, consul d'Alep, d'Alger, de Tripoli, et autres échelles du Levant, tome 3* (Paris).

Lehmann, L.Th., 1991. 'Variations in boatbuilding under the Roman Empire'. In R. Reinders and K. Paul (eds), *Carvel Construction Technique. Skeleton-first, Shell-first. Fifth International Symposium on Boat and Ship Archaeology, Amsterdam 1988* (Oxbow Monograph 12, Oxford), 24-7.

Lepelley, C., 1981. *Les cités de l'Afrique romaine au bas-empire*, tome II (Paris).

Bibliography

Liebeschuetz, J.H.W.G., 1972. *Antioch. City and Imperial Administration in the Later Roman Empire* (Oxford).

Ligt, L. de, 1993. *Fairs and Markets in the Roman Empire* (Amsterdam).

Linder, E., 1993. 'Ma'agan Michael (the shipwreck)'. In E. Stern (ed.), *The New Encyclopedia of Archaeological Excavations in the Holy Land*, vol. 3 (Jerusalem), 918-19.

Lloyd, M., 1984. *A Byzantine Shipwreck at Iskandil Burnu, Turkey: Preliminary Report* (MA thesis, Texas A&M University).

Long, L. and Sourisseau, J-C, 2002. 'Épave *Grand Ribaud F*, Giens'. In L. Long, P. Pomey and J-C Sourisseau (ed.), *Les Étrusques en Mer. Épaves d'Antibes à Marseille* (Édisud, Marseille), 55-62.

Long, L. and Volpe, G., 1998. 'Le chargement de l'épave 1 de la Palud (VIe s.) à Port-Cros (Var). Note préliminaire'. In M. Bonifay, M.-B. Carre and Y. Rigoir (eds), *Fouilles à Marseille. Les mobiliers (Ier-VIIe siècles ap. J.-C.)* (Études Massaliètes, Paris), 317-42.

Lopez, R.S., 1959. 'The role of trade in the economic readjustment of Byzantium in the 7th century'. *DOP* 13, 69-85.

Maeir, A.M., 1994. 'The excavations at Mamilla, Jerusalem, Phase I (1989)'. In H. Geva (ed.), *Ancient Jerusalem Revealed* (Jerusalem).

Magness, 1992. 'The Late Roman and Byzantine pottery from Areas H and K'. In A. de Groot and D.T. Ariel (ed.), *Excavations at the City of David 1978-1985*, vol. III: *Stratigraphical, Environmental, and other Reports* (Qedem 33, Jerusalem), 149-64.

Magness, J., 2002. *The Archaeology of Qumran and the Dead Sea Scrolls* (Eerdmans).

Maioli, M.G. and Stoppiani, M., 1989. 'Classe, podere chiavichetta: anfore di importazione'. In *Amphores Romaines et histoire économique: dix ans de recherche* (Ecole Française de Rome, Rome), 572-3.

Majcherek, G., 1992. 'The Late Roman ceramics from Sector "G" (Alexandria 1986-1987)'. *Études et Travaux* 16, 81-117.

Manning, S.W., Bolger, D.L., Swinton, A. and Ponting, M.J., 1994. 'Maroni Valley Archaeological Survey Project. Preliminary Report on 1992-1993 Seasons'. *RDAC*, 345-55.

Marcus, R., 1963. *Josephus VIII. Jewish Antiquities, Books XV-XVII* (Cambridge, Mass.).

Martin, A, 1998. 'Ceramica commune tardoantica da Ostia e Porto (V-VII secolo). 1.2. I contesti di Pianabella (Ostia) e Porto: datazione e caratterizzazione'. In L. Saguì (ed.), *Ceramica in Italia: VI-VII* secolo. *Atti del Convegno in onore di John W. Hayes Roma, 11-13 maggio 1995* (Firenze), 386-91.

Mattingly, D.J., 1988a. 'The olive boom. Oil surpluses, wealth and power in Roman Tripolitania'. *Libyan Studies* 19, 21-41.

Mattingly, D.J., 1988b. 'Oil for export? A comparison of Libyan, Spanish and Tunisian olive oil production in the Roman Empire'. *JRA* 1, 33-56.

Mayerson, P., 1985. 'The wine and vineyards of Gaza in the Byzantine period'. *BASOR* 257, 75-80.

Mazar, G., 1981. 'The wine presses of the Negev'. *Qadmoniot* 14, 51-60. (Hebrew.)

Mazor, G. and Bar-Nathan, R., 1998. 'The Bet She'an Excavation Project – 1992-1994. Antiquities Authority Expedition'. *ESI* 17, 7-35.

McCann, A.M. and Freed., J., 1994. *Deep Water Archaeology: a Late-Roman Ship from Carthage and an Ancient Trade Route near Skerki Bank off Northwest Sicily* (JRA Suppl. 13, Michigan).

McCaslin, D., 1978. *Hala Sultan Tekke 4. The 1977 Underwater Report* (Studies in Mediterranean Archaeology XLV.4, Goteborg).

McNicoll, A.W., Edwards, P.C., Hanbury-Tenison, J., Hennessy, J.B., Potts, T.F., Smith, R.H., Walmsley, A. and Watson, P., 1992. *Pella in Jordan 2* (Mediterranean Archaeology Suppl. 2, Sydney).

Meyers, E.M., Meyers, C.L. and Hoglund, G., 1995. 'Sepphoris (Sippori), 1994'. *IEJ* 45, 68-71.

Misch-Brandl, O. and Galili, E., 1985. *From the Depths of the Sea. Cargoes of Ancient Wrecks from the Carmel Coast* (Jerusalem).

Monks, G.R., 1953. 'The Church of Alexandria and the city's economic life in the sixth century'. *Speculum* 28, 349-62.

Monro, V., 1835. *A Summer Ramble in Syria, with a Tartar Trip from Aleppo to Stambal* (London).

Mor, H., 2002-3. 'The Dor (Tantura) 2001/1 Shipwreck. A Preliminary Report'. *RIMS Newsletter* 29, 15-17.

Morris, C.E. and Peatfield, A.A.D., 1987. 'Pottery from the Cyprus Underwater Survey, 1983'. *RDAC*, 199-212.

Mundell Mango, M., 2001. 'Beyond the amphora: non-ceramic evidence for Late Antique industry and trade'. In S. Kingsley and M. Decker (eds), *Economy and Exchange in the East Mediterranean during Late Antiquity* (Oxford), 87-106.

Neale, F.A., 1852. *Eight Years in Syria, Palestine and Asia Minor from 1842 to 1850*, vol. I (London).

Neev, D. and Ben-Avraham, Z., 1977. 'The Levantine countries: the

Bibliography

Israeli coastal region'. In A.E.M. Nairn, W.H. Kanes and F.G. Stehli (eds), *The Ocean Basins and Margins*, vol. 4a: *The Eastern Mediterranean* (London), 355-77.

Negev, N., 1997. 'Nahal Hevron – Dams'. *ESI* 16, 128-31.

Nir, Y., 1982a. 'Offshore artificial structures and their influence on the Israel and Sinai Mediterranean beaches'. In *Proceedings of the Eighteenth Coastal Engineering Conference ASCE* (Cape Town), 1837-56.

Nir, Y., 1982b. 'Asia, Middle East, Coastal morphology: Israel and Sinai'. In M.L. Schwartz (ed.), *The Encyclopedia of Beaches and Coastal Environments* (Pennsylvania), 86-98.

Nir, Y., 1990. 'Twenty-five years of development along the Israeli Mediterranean coast: goals and achievements'. In P. Fabbri (ed.), *Recreational Uses of Coastal Areas* (Netherlands), 211-18.

Oked, S., 1996. 'Patterns of the transport amphorae at Ostrakine during the 6th and 7th Centuries'. *ARAM* 8, 165-75.

Oleson, J.P., 1988. 'Ancient lead circles and sounding-leads from Israeli coastal waters'. *Sefunim* 7, 27-40.

Oleson, J.P., Fitzgerald, M.A., Sherwood, A.N. and Sidebotham, S.E., 1994. *The Harbours of Caesarea Maritima. Results of the Caesarea Ancient Harbour Excavation Project 1980-85*, vol. II: *The Find and the Ship* (BAR Int. Series 594, Oxford).

Oleson, J.P., Hohlfelder, R.L., Raban, A. and Vann, R.L., 1984. 'The Caesarea Ancient Harbour Excavation Project (CAHEP): Preliminary Report on the 1980-1983 Seasons'. *JFA* 11, 281-305.

Opait, A., 1998. 'New pottery from the circular harbour of Carthage'. *CEDAC* 18, 21-35.

Ovadiah, A., 1969. 'Excavations in the area of the Ancient Synagogue at Gaza (Preliminary Report)'. *IEJ* 19, 193-98.

Ovadiah, A., 1993. 'Early churches'. In E. Stern (ed.) *The New Encyclopedia of Archaeological Excavations in the Holy Land*, vol. 1 (Jerusalem), 305-9.

Owen, R., 1981. *The Middle East in the World Economy 1800-1914* (London).

Parker, A.J., 1979. 'Method and madness: wreck hunting in shallow water'. In J.C. Gamble and J.D. George (eds), *Progress in Underwater Science*, vol. 4 (London), 7-27.

Parker, A.J., 1981. 'Stratification and contamination in Ancient Mediterranean shipwrecks'. *IJNA* 10, 309-35.

Parker, A.J., 1984. 'Shipwrecks and ancient trade in the Mediterranean'. *Archaeological Review from Cambridge* 3, 99-107.

Bibliography

Parker, A.J., 1990. 'Classical Antiquity: the maritime dimension'. *Antiquity* 64, 335-46.

Parker, A.J., 1992a. *Ancient Shipwrecks of the Mediterranean and the Roman Provinces* (BAR Int. Series 580, Oxford).

Parker, A.J., 1992b. 'Cargoes, containers and stowage: the Ancient Mediterranean'. *IJNA* 21, 89-100.

Peacock, D.P.S., 1984. 'The amphorae: typology and chronology'. In M.G. Fulford and D.P.S. Peacock (ed.), *The Avenue de President Habib Bourguiba, Salammbo: the Pottery and other Ceramic Objects from the Site*, vol. 1.2 (Sheffield), 116-40.

Peacock, D.P.S., Bejaoui, F. and Ben Lazreg, N., 1989. 'Roman amphora production in the Sahel region of Tunisia'. In *Amphores romaines et histoire économique: dix ans de recherche* (Rome), 179-222.

Peacock, D.P.S. and Williams, D.F., 1986. *Amphorae and the Roman Economy* (London).

Pederson, R.K., 2000. 'Under the Erythraean Sea: an ancient shipwreck in Eritrea'. *INA Quarterly* 27.2/3, 3-12.

Peleg, M. and Reich, R., 1992. 'Excavations of a segment of the Byzantine city wall of Caesarea Maritima'. *'Atiqot* 21, 137-70.

Pharr, C., 1952. *The Theodosian Code and Novels and the Simondian Constitutions* (Princeton).

Plat Taylor, J. du and Megaw, A.H.S., 1981. 'Excavations at Ayios Philon, the Ancient Carpasia. Part II: the Early Christian Buildings'. *RDAC*, 209-50.

Pomey, P., 1994. 'Shell conception and skeleton process in Ancient Mediterranean shipbuilding'. In C. Westerdahl (ed.), *Crossroads in Ancient Shipbuilding. Proceedings of the Sixth International Symposium on Boat and Ship Archaeology Roskilde 1991* (Oxford), 125-30.

Prausnitz, M.W., 1967. *Excavations at Shavei Zion* (Rome).

Presle, A.D. de la, 1993. 'Inscriptions grecques sur deux balances romaines trouvées à Dor'. *Revue Biblique* 4, 580-8.

Raban, A., 1969-71. 'The finds from the undersea site of Hof HaCarmel'. *Sefunim* 3, 62-9.

Raban, A., 1971. 'The shipwreck off Sharm-el-Sheikh'. *Archaeology* 24, 146-55.

Raban, A., 1973. 'Survival of ancient wrecks in various conditions off the coast near Israel'. In N. Flemming (ed.) *Science Diving International* (London), 29-39.

Raban, A., 1985. 'The ancient harbours of Israel in Biblical times'. In

Bibliography

A. Raban (ed.), *Harbour Archaeology* (BAR Int. Series 257, Oxford), 11-44.

Raban, A., 1989. *The Harbors of Caesarea Maritima. Results of the Caesarea Ancient Harbor Excavation Project, 1980-1985*, vol. I: *The Site and the Excavations* (BAR Int. Series 491, Oxford).

Raban, A., 1992. 'Sebastos: the Royal Harbour at Caesarea Maritima – a short-lived giant'. *IJNA* 21, 111-24.

Raban, A., 1995. 'Dor-Yam: maritime and coastal installations at Dor in their geomorphological and stratigraphic context'. In E. Stern, *Excavations at Dor, Final Report*, vol. IA: *Areas A and C: Introduction and Stratigraphy* (Jerusalem), 285-354.

Raban, A., Holum, K.G. and Blakely, J.A., 1993. *The Combined Caesarea Expeditions. Field Report of the 1992 Season* (University of Haifa).

Raban, A. and Linder, E., 1993. 'Maritime 'Atlit'. In E. Stern (ed.), *The New Encyclopedia of Archaeological Excavations in the Holy Land*, vol. 3 (Jerusalem), 117-20.

Rautman, M.L., Gomez, B., Neff, H. and Glascock, M.D., 1993. 'Neutron activation analysis of Late Roman ceramics from Kalavasos-*Kopetra* and the environs of the Vasilikos Valley'. *RDAC*, 233-64.

Raveh, K. and Kingsley, S., 1991. 'The status of Dor in Late Antiquity: a maritime perspective'. *Biblical Archaeologist* 54, 198-207.

Raven, S., 1984. *Rome in Africa* (London).

Reynolds, P., 1995. *Trade in the Western Mediterranean, AD 400-700: the Ceramic Evidence* (BAR Int. Series 604, Oxford).

Reynolds, P., 1997-8. 'Pottery production and economic exchange in second century Berytus: some preliminary observations of ceramic trends from quantified ceramic deposits from the Aub-Leverhulme excavations in Beirut'. *Berytus* 43, 35-110.

Rickman, G.E., 1980. 'The grain trade under the Roman Empire'. In J.H. d'Arms and E.C. Kopff (eds), *The Seaborne Commerce of Ancient Rome: Studies in Archaeology and History* (Rome), 261-76.

Riley, J., 1979. 'The coarse pottery from Benghazi'. In J.A. Lloyd (ed.), *Sidi Khrebish Excavations. Benghazi (Berenice)*, vol. II (Tripoli), 91-449.

Riley, J.A., 1981. 'The pottery from the cisterns 1977.1, 1977.2, 1977.3'. In J.H. Humphrey (ed.), *Excavations at Carthage 1977, Conducted by the University of Michigan*, vol. VI (Ann Arbor), 85-124.

Bibliography

Roll, I. and Ayalon, E., 1989. *Apollonia and Southern Sharon. Model of a Coastal City* (Tel Aviv). (Hebrew.)

Ronen, A. and Olami, Y., 1978. *'Atlit Map* (Jerusalem).

Ronen, A. and Zemer, A., 1981. 'A structure of shells near Ashqelon'. *Qadmoniot* 14, 47-50. (Hebrew.)

Ross, M.C., 1962. *Catalogue of the Byzantine and Early Mediaeval Antiquities in the Dumbarton Oaks Collection*, vol. 1: *Metalwork, Ceramics, Glass, Glyptics, Painting* (Washington).

Rougé, J., 1966. *Totius Mundi et Gentium* (Paris).

Safrai, Z., 1994. *The Economy of Roman Palestine* (London).

Sams, G.K., 1982. 'The weighing implements'. In G.F. Bass and F.H. van Doorninck (eds), *Yassi Ada I. A Seventh-Century Byzantine Shipwreck* (Texas), 202-30.

Santamaria, C., 1995. *L'épave Dramont E à Saint-Raphael (Ve siècle ap. J.-C.)* (Archaeonautica 13, Paris).

Schnelz, U.O., 1990. 'Population characteristics of Jerusalem and Hebron regions according to Ottoman census of 1905'. In G.G. Gilbar (ed.), *Ottoman Palestine 1800-1914. Studies in Economic and Social History* (Leiden), 15-67.

Schölch, A., 1982. 'European penetration and the economic development of Palestine, 1856-82'. In R. Owen (ed.), *Studies in the Economic and Social History of Palestine in the Nineteenth and Twentieth Centuries* (Oxford), 10-87.

Schwartz, J.J., 1991. *Lod (Lydda), Israel* (BAR Int. Series 571, Oxford).

Schwartz, J.J., 1998. 'Archaeology and the city'. In D. Sperber, *The City in Roman Palestine* (Oxford), 149-87.

Scorpan, C., 1977. 'Contribution à la connaissance de certains types céramiques Romano-Byzantins (IV-VII siècles) dans l'espace Istro-Pontique'. *Dacia* 21, 269-97.

Sedov, A.V., 1992. 'New archaeological and epigraphical material from Qana (South Arabia)'. *Arabian Archaeology and Epigraphy* 3, 110-35.

Segrè, A., 1943. 'Essays on Byzantine economic history, I. The *annona civica* and the *annona militaris*'. *Byzantion* 16, 393-444.

Seligman, J., 1994. 'Jerusalem, Pisgat Ze'ev (East A)'. *ESI* 12, 52-4.

Shanks, H. (ed.), 1996. *Archaeology's Publication Problem* (Washington).

Shanks, H. (ed.), 1999. *Archaeology's Publication Problem*, vol. 2 (Washington).

Bibliography

Shereshevski, J., 1991. *Byzantine Urban Settlements in the Negev Desert* (Beer-Sheva V, Ben-Gurion).

Shourkin, O., 1997. 'Jerusalem, Pisgat Ze'ev E'. *ESI* 16, 99.

Sibella, P., 1995a. 'The ceramics'. *The INA Quarterly* 22, 13-16.

Sibella, P., 1995b. 'Notes on the architectural marble'. *The INA Quarterly* 22, 19-20.

Siegelmann, A., 1974. 'A mosaic floor at Caesarea Maritima'. *IEJ* 24, 216-21.

Sirks, B., 1991a. *Food for Rome. The Legal Structure of the Transportation and Processing of Supplies for the Imperial Distributions in Rome and Constantinople* (Amsterdam).

Sirks, A.J.B., 1991b. 'The size of the grain distributions in Imperial Rome and Constantinople'. *Athenaeum* 11, 215-37.

Smith., G.A., 1894. *The Historical Geography of the Holy Land* (London).

Sodini, J.-P., 1989. 'Le commerce des marbres à l'époque protobyzantine'. In *Hommes et richesses dans l'Empire byzantin*, tome I: IVe-VIIe siècle (Paris), 162-86.

Solier, Y, 1981. *Les épaves de Gruissan* (Archaeonautica 3, Paris).

Southern, P. and Dixon, K.R., 1996. *The Late Roman Army* (London).

Sperber, D., 1970. 'On social and economic conditions in third century Palestine'. *Archiv Orientalni* 38, 1-25.

Sperber, D., 1978. *Roman Palestine, 200-400. The Land. Crisis and Change in Agrarian Society as Reflected in Rabbinic Sources* (Ramat Gan).

Sperber, D., 1986. *Nautica Talmudica* (Bar Ilan University Press).

St Thackeray, H., 1966. *Josephus I. The Life. Against Apion* (Cambridge, Mass., 4th ed.).

Steffy, J.R., 1990. 'The boat: a preliminary study of its construction'. In S. Wachsmann, *The Excavations of an Ancient Boat in the Sea of Galilee (Lake Kinneret)*, ('Atiqot 19, Jerusalem), 29-48.

Steffy, R., 1991. 'The Mediterranean shell to skeleton transition: a northwest European parallel?'. In R. Reinders and K. Paul (ed.), *Carvel Construction Technique. Skeleton-first, Shell-first. Fifth International Symposium on Boat and Ship Archaeology, Amsterdam 1988* (Oxbow Monograph 12, Oxford), 1-9.

Steffy, J.R., 1994. *Wooden Ship Building and the Interpretation of Shipwrecks* (Texas).

Steffy, J.R., 1995. 'Ancient scantlings: the projection and control of Mediterranean hull shapes'. In H. Tzalas (ed.), *Third International*

Symposium on Ship Construction in Antiquity. Tropis III (Thessaloniki), 417-28.

Stephens, G., 1838. *Incidents of Travel in Egypt, Arabia Petraea and the Holy Land*, vol. II (London).

Stephens Crawford, J., 1990. *The Byzantine Shops at Sardis* (Cambridge, Mass.).

Stewart, R.W., 1857. *The Tent and the Khan: a Journey to Sinai and Palestine* (London).

Storey G.R., 1999. 'Archaeology and Roman society: integrating textual and archaeological data'. *Journal of Archaeological Research* 7, 203-48.

Syon, D., 1998. 'A wine press at Akhziv'. *'Atiqot* 34, 85-99. (Hebrew.)

Tahal, G., 1995. 'Avedat'. *ESI* 14, 130-3.

Tchernia, A., 1986. *Le vin de l'Italie romaine. Essai d'histoire economique d'après les amphores* (Rome).

Teall, J.L., 1959. 'The grain supply of the Byzantine Empire, 330-1025'. *DOP* 13, 89-139.

Throckmorton, P. and Throckmorton, J., 1973. 'The Roman wreck at Pantano Longarini'. *IJNA* 2, 243-66.

Tomber, R.S., 1988a. *Pottery in Long-Distance Economic Inference: an Investigation of Methodology with Reference to Roman Carthage* (PhD thesis, University of Southampton).

Tomber, R.S., 1988b. 'Pottery from the 1982-83 Excavations'. In J.H. Humphrey (ed.), *The Circus and a Byzantine Cemetery at Carthage*, vol. I (Michigan), 437-538.

Tomber, R.S., 1996. 'Provisioning the desert: pottery supply to Mons Claudianus'. In D.M. Bailey (ed.), *Archaeological Research in Roman Egypt. The Proceedings of the Seventeenth Classical Colloquium of the Department of Greek and Roman Antiquities, British Museum* (JRA Suppl. 19, Ann Arbor), 39-49.

Tubb, J.N., 1986. 'The pottery from a Byzantine well near Tell Fara'. *PEQ*, 51-65.

Treadgold, W., 1995. *Byzantium and its Army* (Palo Alto).

Tristram, H.B., 1866. *The Land of Israel; a Journal of Travels in Palestine* (London, 2nd ed.).

Tsafrir, Y., 1996. 'Some notes on the settlement and demography of Palestine in the Byzantine period: the archaeological evidence'. In J.D. Seger (ed.), *Retrieving the Past. Essays on Archaeological Research and Methodology in Honor of Gus W. van Beek* (Mississippi), 269-83.

Tsafrir, Y. and Foerster, G., 1994. 'From Scythopolis to Baysan –

changing concepts of urbanism'. In G.R.D. King and A. Cameron (ed.), *The Byzantine and Early Islamic Near East II. Land Use and Settlement Patterns* (New Jersey), 95-116.

Tsuk, T. and Ayalon, E., 1995. 'Herziliya Tunnel'. *ESI* 14, 140-1.

Tzaferis, V. and Peleg, M., 1990. 'Kefar Nahum – 1986/1987'. *ESI* 7-8, 108-9.

Ullmann, L. and Galili, E., 1994. 'A Greek inscription mentioning Sucamina discovered off the Carmel coast'. *Scripta Classica Israelica* 13, 116-22.

Urman, D., 1985. *The Golan. A Profile of a Region during the Roman and Byzantine Periods* (BAR Int. Series 269, Oxford).

Van Alfen, P.G., 1996. 'New light on the 7th-c. Yassi Ada shipwreck. Capacities and standard sizes of LRA1 amphoras'. *JRA* 9, 189-213.

Van Doorninck, F.H, 1982a. 'The hull remains'. In G.F. Bass and F.H. van Doorninck (eds), *Yassi Ada I. A Seventh-Century Byzantine Shipwreck* (Texas), 32-63.

Van Doorninck, F.H., 1982b. 'The anchors'. In G.F. Bass and F.H. van Doorninck (eds), *Yassi Ada I. A Seventh-Century Byzantine Shipwreck* (Texas), 121-41.

Van Doorninck, F.H, 1982c. 'An 11th century shipwreck at Serçe Liman, Turkey: 1978-81'. *IJNA* 11, 7-11.

Van Doorninck, F.H., 1988. 'The glass wreck at Serçe Limani. The anchors: a limited technology, a sophisticated design'. *INA Newsletter* 15, 24-5.

Villedieu, F., 1984. *Turris Libisonis. Fouille d'un site romain tardif à Porto Torres, Sardaigne* (BAR Int. Series 224, Oxford).

Vitto, F., 1996. 'Byzantine mosaics at Bet She'arim: new evidence for the history of the site'. *'Atiqot* 28, 115-46.

Wachsmann, S., 1984-5. 'Nautical archaeological inspection by the Israel Department of Antiquities and Museums'. *BAIAS,* 24-9.

Wachsmann, S., 1990. *The Excavations of an Ancient Boat in the Sea of Galilee (Lake Kinneret)* ('Atiqot 19, Jerusalem).

Wachsmann, S., 1996. 'A cove of many shipwrecks: the 1995 INA/CMS Joint Expedition to Tantura Lagoon'. *CMS News* 23, 17-21.

Wachsmann, S. and Davis, D., 2002. 'Nautical archaeology in Israel'. In C.V. Ruppé and J.F. Barstad (ed.), *International Handbook of Underwater Archaeology* (New York), 499-518.

Wachsmann, S. and Kahanov, Y., 1997. 'The 1995 INA/CMS Joint Expedition to Tantura Lagoon, Israel'. *The INA Quarterly* 24, 3-18.

Wachsmann, S., Kahanov, Y. and Hall, J., 1997. 'The *Tantura B*

Bibliography

Shipwreck: the 1996 INA/CMS Joint Expedition to Tantura Lagoon'. *INA Quarterly* 24, 3-18.

Wachsmann, S. and Raveh, K., 1985. 'Hahotrim coast, shipwreck'. *ESI* 3, 37.

Ward-Perkins, B., 2000. 'Specialized production and exchange'. In A. Cameron, B. Ward-Perkins and M. Whitby (eds), *The Cambridge Ancient History*, vol. XIV: *Late Antiquity: Empire and Successors, AD 425-600* (Cambridge), 346-91.

Weinberg, S.S., 1988. 'The buildings and installations'. In G.D. Weinberg (ed.), *Excavations at Jalame. Site of a Glass Factory in Late Roman Palestine* (Columbia), 5-23.

Weinberg, G.D. and Goldstein, S.M., 1988. 'The glass vessels'. In G.D. Weinberg (ed.), *Excavations at Jalame. Site of a Glass Factory in Late Roman Palestine* (Columbia), 38-102.

Whitby, M., 1995. 'Recruitment in Roman armies from Justinian to Heraclius (c. 565-615)'. In A. Cameron (ed.), *The Byzantine and Early Islamic Near East III. States, Resources and Armies* (New Jersey), 61-124.

Whitcomb, 1995. 'Islam and the socio-cultural transition of Palestine – Early Islamic Period (638-1099 CE)'. In T.E. Levy (ed.), *The Archaeology of Society in the Holy Land* (Leicester), 482-501.

Whitcomb, D., forthcoming. 'The "commercial crescent". Red Sea trade in Late Antiquity and Early Islam'. In *Late Antiquity and Early Islam. Fifth Workshop. Trade and Exchange in the Late Antique and Early Islamic Near East*.

Whitehouse, D., Constantini, L., Guidobaldi, F., Passi, S., Pensabene, P., Pratt, S., Reese, R. and Reese, D., 1985. 'The Schola Praeconum II'. *PBSR* 53, 163-209.

Whittaker, C.R., 1976. '*Agri Deserti*'. In M.I. Finley (ed.), *Studies in Roman Property* (Cambridge), 137-200.

Whittaker, C.R., 1983. 'Late Roman trade and traders'. In P. Garnsey, K. Hopkins and C.R. Whittaker (eds), *Trade in the Ancient Economy* (London), 163-80.

Wickham, C., 1988. 'Marx, Sherlock Holmes and Late Roman commerce'. *JRS* 78, 183-93.

Williams, D., 2002. 'A note on the petrology of pottery and tile from the Dor D Wreck'. In S.A. Kingsley, *A Sixth-Century AD Shipwreck off the Carmel Coast, Israel. Dor D and Holy Land Wine Trade* (BAR Int. Series 1065, Oxford), 111-2.

Wilson, C.T., 1906. *Peasant Life in the Holy Land* (London).

Wortley, J. (trans), 1992. *The Spiritual Meadow* (Michigan).

Bibliography

Zemer, A., 1977. *Storage Jars in Ancient Sea Trade* (Haifa).
Zevulun, U. and Olenik, Y., 1979. *Function and Design in the Talmudic Period* (Tel Aviv, 2nd. ed).

Index

Aba, Rabbi, 127
Abu Mena (Egypt), 118
Achziv (town, Galilee), wine press, 90
African Red Slip (ARS), pottery, 19, 70, 110, 119, 121, 122
Agios Georgios (Cyprus), 96
Akko (port, Israel), 23, 24, 30-2, 39, 42, 81, 123, 127
Alexandria, Christian see, 70, 73, 94, 122
amphorae, Cape Andreas (Cyprus), 52; Carmel Beach 1 (HC1), 46, 50, 69; carrot-shaped (Black Sea/Syrian), 105; Coptic, 105; Egyptian, 105; Hala Sultan Tekke (Cyprus), 52; imports, to Palestine, 50, 102-9; Keay I, 46, 50; Keay XXVG, 105; Keratidhi Bay (Cyprus), 52; LR1 (Syrian/Cypriot), 46, 54, 105, 117; LR2 (Aegean), 46, 50, 105, 117; LR3 (Asia Minor), 105; LR4 (Palestinian), 46, 51, 84, 92; export levels, 94-102; import levels, 118; LR5 (Palestinian), 24, 46, 51, 58, 61, 92; export levels, 94-102; recycling, 47; Serçe Limani (Turkey), 52; Spanish, 17; Tunisian, 18, 120
Anastasius I, 116, 121
anchors, iron 56; stone, 57-8
annona civica, Roman tax in kind, 17-19, 61, 70, 115-16
annona militaris, Roman military tax, 113-15
Antesion (Israel), 78
Antioch, 122, 126
Apollonia (port, Israel), 21, 29, 48, 56, 79, 81
Aquileia, 122
Arab conquest, 56
Archaeological Survey of Israel, 21
Arles, 94, 98, 120
Ashdod (port, Israel), 29
Ashkelon (port, Israel), 21, 29, 83; wine press, 88
Athens, 94
Atlit (port, Israel), 25, 68; Hellenistic ram, 130
Avi-Yonah, Michael, 76
Ayia Varvara (Cyprus), 54
Ayios Philon (Cyprus), 99

Ballana (lower Egypt), 94
ballast, 51, 54
Barcino (Spain), 120
Bass, George, 13, 128

Index

Beirut, 116, 120
Belisarius, fleet, 72
Benalua (Spain), 96
Bet Eli'ezer (glass kilns, Israel), 82
Beth Shearim (town, Galilee), 81, 105
Biblical Archaeology Society, 129
Buckingham, J.S., 30

Caesarea (port, Israel), 21, 24, 56, 81; dyeworks, 84; inscriptions, 78; pottery imports, 107, 109, 119
Calle Soledad (Spain), 96, 98
Caparbaricha (monastery, Judaea), wine press, 90
Capernaum, dyeworks (town, Galilee), 83
Carmel, beaches (Israel), 28, 43
Carthage (Libya), 94, 116, 122; amphora imports, 98-100, 113, 120
Chevalier d'Arvieux, 39
Chios, 96, 99, 117
Choricius, 126
Christian, shipping, 47, 59
cloth dyeing, 83-6
Constantine I, 113
Constantinople, 62, 70, 96, 99, 122; tax, 116
Corinth, 94
Crete, 9
Cultural Resource Management, 10
Cunningham Geikie, 31
Cypriot Red Slip (CRS), pottery, 54, 110, 119, 121
Cyzicos, 122

Dabiyye (Golan), 110

Dah-Dah, Khirbet (farm, Hebron), 83
Danube, 96
Dead Sea Scrolls, 131
Dever, William, 129
Diospolis (city, Israel), dyeworks, 84
domestic assemblage, 46, 52-6
Dor (port, Israel), 21, 56, 79; pottery imports, 119

Eboda (Negev), wine press, 88
Egyptian Red-Slip (ERS), pottery, 110
'Ein Hazeva (Israel), 102
Elusa (Negev), wine press, 88
Emporiae (Spain), 96, 120
Eulogius of Alexandria, 113
Expositio Totius Mundi et Gentium, 82, 84

Fara, Tel (Negev), 107
frame first (shipbuilding technique), 65

Gaza (port, Israel), 21, 68, 123; dyeworks, 83; festival of St Sergius, 126
Gazit (Galilee, Israel), 21
George, son of Ision, 59
Gibraltar, 9
glass, 80-3
Golan, 75
Gregory the Great, 113
Guadalquivir Valley (Andalucia), 17
Gush Halav (Galilee), 105, 121

Hadera (Sharon Plain), 29
Haifa (port, Israel), 28, 31, 32, 39, 42, 48, 123, 124

Index

Halicarnassus, 106
Hammat Gader (Israel), 102
Hauran, 123, 124
Hazor, Tell (Israel), 130
Heraclea, 122
Herzog, Ze'ev, 130
Hilal, Khirbet (farmstead, Jerusalem), 88, 89
Histria (Black Sea), 96
Horvat Qav (Israel), 80

Israel Antiquities Authority (IAA), 26, 27, 69, 74, 131
Israel Department of Antiquities, 26, 27

Jaffa (port, Israel), 23, 30, 36
Jalame (estate, Israel), 81; pottery imports, 107; wine press, 88
Jerusalem, 76, 82, 88
Jews, merchants, 70, 83-4; pottery import, 110; trade, 127; viticulture, 61
Jezreel Valley (Israel), 21
John Malalas, 115
Jones, A.H.M., 75
Jordan, 19
Josephus Flavius, 23, 35
Jules Verne, 13
Justinian, 114
Justinianic plague, 56, 69, 127-8
Juvenal (Roman satirist), 9

Kalavasos-Kopetra (Cyprus), 96
Kfar Hananya (Galilee), pottery, 120
Kishon, river (Israel), 31
Korazin (Galilee), 121
Kyrios Leontis, synagogue of (Galilee), 105

Libanius, of Antioch, 126
limitanei, frontier troops, 114
Link Expedition, 24
Lod, 75
Lyon, 94

Marseille, 96, 98; pottery imports, 113, 120
Masira Island (Oman), 94
Maskhuta, Tell el- (Egypt), 96
Meiron (Galilee), 105
Monastil, El (Spain), 96
Mons Claudianus (Egypt), 96
Monte Testaccio, amphora deposits, 17
mortise and tenons (shipbuilding technique) 9, 63, 65
Moschos, John, 73
Mount Hermon (Golan), 19
murex, 83

Nahariyya (town, Israel), 88
Naples, 94, 98, 120
Narbonne, 94
Neapolis (city, Israel), dyeworks, 84
Negev, desert, 21, 79, 110, 118; dams, 79; wine presses, 88
Neve Yam (anchorage, Israel), 43
Nicomedia, 122
Nile, 118; sediments, 35, 68

Ohad (Negev), 118
Ostia, 9, 76, 94
Ostrakina (Sinai), 99
Ottoman, 124
Oxyrhynchos (town, Egypt), cloth manufacture, 85

Index

Palaestina, Byzantine province, 19-22, 60, 80, 88; amphora imports, 102-10
Paphos, 54
Parker, A.J., 14
Pella (Jordan), 94
Pergamon (Turkey), 94
periploi, nautical handbooks, 9
Petrera (Cyprus), 96
Phocaean Red Slip (PRS), pottery, 110, 119, 121
Phocas, emperor, 116, 121
Phoenicia, dyeworks, 85
Pisgat Ze'ev (monastery, Israel), 90
Plaza de los Tres Reyes (Spain), 96
Porto Torres (Sardinia), 96
Proconnesian marble, 60, 61
Psates of Rhion, 59

Qana (Yemen), 94
Qasile, Tel (Tel Aviv), wine press, 89
Qatsrin (Israel), 121

Rakit, Horvat (estate, Galilee), 81
Ravenna, 94
Recanati Institute for Maritime Studies, Haifa, 26
Remotely Operated Vehicles, 10, 14, 131
Rhodas (Spain), 120
Rhodes, 9
Rhodian Sea Law, 9, 42
Rome, 94; amphora imports, 101-2
roof tiles, 54
Rosh Hanniqra (north Israel), 42

Saewulf, twelfth-century pilgrim, 36
Sahel (Tunisia), olive oil, 18
Samaria, 75
Samaritans, 102
San Giovanni di Ruoti, 96
Saraçhane, (Turkey) 54, 96, 116
Sardis, 54, 94, 106, 117
Schola Praeconum, Rome, 98
Scuba, 24, 28
Scythopolis (city, Galilee), 81-2, 84-5
Sdot Yam (anchorage, Israel), 29
Sepphoris (city, Galilee), 82
Shefarim (Israel), 21
Shelomi (Galilee), 102, 110
Shema, Khirbet (Galilee), 105
shipwrecks, Apollonia (Israel), 29; Ashkelon (Israel), 29, 48, 67, 131; Atlit (Israel), 48, 49, 51; Black Sea, 9, 15, 32; Caesarea (Israel), 26, 39, 50, 68, 130; Carmel Beach, 43, 50; Corfu, 52; Dor (Israel), 26, 37-44, 48, 50, 51, 54, 56-61, 66-9, 71, 72, 126, 130; Dover (England), 15; Dramont E (France), 65, 117; Dramont F (France), 64; Erythraean Sea, 15; Femmina Morta (Sicily), 65; Ginosar B (Israel), 67; Givat Olga (Israel), 50; Grand basin D (France), 66; Grand Ribaud A (France), 14; Greece, 10; Hahotrim (Israel), 60, 131; Héliopolis A (France), 66; Iskandil Burnu (Turkey), 72; Kekova Oludeniz (Turkey), 52; Kizilagac Adasi (Turkey), 52;

Index

La Palud (France), 52, 102;
Le Scole A (Italy), 73;
Ma'agan Michael (Israel), 26, 39, 130; *Mary Rose*, 10;
Marzamemi (Sicily), 15, 60;
Megadim (Israel), 131; Neve Yam (Israel), 43; Newport (Wales), 10; Pantano Longarini (Sicily), 65, 73;
Porticello (Sicily), 15;
quantities lost, 29-33;
recycled cargoes, 48, 56-8;
salvage, 42; Sdot Yam (Israel), 48, 50; Sea of Galilee (Israel), 26; Serçe Limani (Turkey), 57, 69; Sharm el Sheikh (Sinai), 26; Sobra (Croatia), 73; St Gervais B (France) 65, 117; Straits of Gibraltar, Punic, 14; Skerki Bank, 14; *Titanic*, 13; Tantura (Dor, Israel), 61, 67; Ulu Burun (Turkey), 14; Yassi Ada A (Turkey), 14, 54, 57, 59, 65, 117
side-scan sonar, 50
Sinai, 19
Smith, George Adam, 24
Sobata (Negev), wine press, 88
sounding leads, 36
steelyards, 59, 60
Sumaqa (Carmel, Israel), 78, 80, 126; coins, 122; pottery imports, 105, 107, 109; wine presses, 90-2
Sycamina (port, Israel), 48, 80

Tarraco (Spain), 96
Tarragona, 98, 120
Tell Hreiz, 48
Temple of Magna Mater, Rome, 98, 120
Theodosian Code, 62, 75, 82, 84, 85, 114, 115
Thessalonica, 122
Troodos Massif (Cyprus), 54

Upper Moesia, 96
Upper Zohar (fort, Negev), 118
urinatores, Roman, 9

Vandals, 117

Wadi Umm Hashim (Negev), 110
wine, production, 86-92; lever and press facilities, 88; screw presses, 88-91
Wroxeter (England), 94

Yavne-Yam (port, Israel), 29, 56
Yohanan, Rabbi, 78

Zenonos, of Ashkelon (tanner), 83
Zikhrin, Khirbet (Israel), 78